THE TRIAL

Harold Pinter was born in East London in 1930.
He is married to Antonia Fraser.

THE TRIAL

adapted from the novel by Franz Kafka

Harold Pinter

faber and faber

LONDON · BOSTON

First published in 1993
by Faber and Faber Limited
3 Queen Square London WC1N 3AU

Photoset by Parker Typesetting Service, Leicester
Printed in England by Clays Ltd, St Ives plc

Harold Pinter is hereby identified as author of this work in accordance with
Section 77 of the Copyright, Designs and Patents Act 1988

The Trial is based on the novel *The Trial* by Franz Kafka,
published by Secker & Warburg Ltd

A CIP record for this book
is available from the British Library

ISBN 0–571–16876–0

2 4 6 8 10 9 7 5 3

To David Jones and Louis Marks

The Trial was made by BBC Films and Europanda Entertainment B.V. The cast included:

JOSEF K	Kyle MacLachlan
THE PRIEST	Anthony Hopkins
DR HULD	Jason Robards
FRÄULEIN BÜRSTNER	Juliet Stevenson
LENI	Polly Walker
TITORELLI	Alfred Molina
BLOCK	Michael Kitchen
K'S UNCLE	Robert Lang
WASHERWOMAN	Catherine Neilson
FRANZ	David Thewlis
WILLEM	Tony Haygarth
INSPECTOR	Douglas Hodge
EXAMINING MAGISTRATE	Trevor Peacock
COURT USHER	Patrick Godfrey
THE FLOGGER	Don Henderson

Directed by	David Jones
Producer	Louis Marks
Screenplay	Harold Pinter
Music Composed and Conducted by	Carl Davis
Associate Producer	Carolyn Montagu
Costume Designer	Anushia Nieradzik
Film Editor	John Stothart
Production Designer	Don Taylor
Director of Photography	Phil Meheux, BSC
Executive Producers	Kobi Jaeger
	Reniero Compostella
	Mark Shivas

Filmed on location and at Barrandov Film Studios, Prague, Czechoslovakia, March–May 1992

Author's Note

This screenplay was shot in its entirety. During the editing of the film, however, a number of scenes were cut. These cuts were made with my approval.

HP

INT. JOSEF K'S BEDROOM. MORNING
*K is in bed, asleep. Low murmurs from another room. Men's voices.
K's eyes open. He lies, listening. He looks up and out of the window.*

WINDOW ACROSS THE STREET. K'S POINT OF VIEW. DAY
*An old woman, holding the curtain, looking across the street into his
window.*

INT. K'S BEDROOM. DAY
*K sits up and looks at the door into the other room. He picks up a bell
and rings it. The voices stop abruptly.*
*The door opens. A man (*FRANZ, *the first warder) comes in.*
JOSEF K: Who are you?
FRANZ: You rang?
JOSEF K: I'm waiting for Anna to bring me my breakfast.
 The man looks back into the other room and speaks to someone.
FRANZ: He says he's waiting for Anna to bring him his breakfast.
 A guffaw from within. The man turns back to K.
 It's not possible.
 *K gets out of bed. He is wearing a nightshirt. He puts on a pair of
 trousers.*
JOSEF K: I'm going to find out what Frau Grubach has to say
 about this.
FRANZ: Listen. I think you'd better stay here.
 K pushes past him and goes into the other room.

INT. K'S SITTING ROOM. DAY
*A second man (*WILLEM, *the second warder) is sitting by the window
reading a book. He looks up.*
WILLEM: You should have stayed in your room. Didn't he tell
 you?
JOSEF K: Who are you? What do you want?
 He looks from one to the other. They study him in silence.
 Through the window K *sees across the street the old lady at her
 window, holding the curtain, looking into the room.*

I

Where's Frau Grubach?

He moves towards the door. WILLEM *stands up.*

WILLEM: You can't go out. You're under arrest.

JOSEF K: Am I? Why?

WILLEM: We're not authorized to tell you. Go to your room and
    wait. Eh, wait a minute, let's have a look at this. That's a
    very nice nightshirt you're wearing. (*To* FRANZ) Isn't it?

FRANZ: It's beautiful.

WILLEM: Listen. We're going to take care of this nightshirt for
    you. You don't mind that, do you? We're going to look after
    all your underwear, in fact. But don't worry. If your case
    turns out all right, you'll get it all back.

FRANZ: You see, it's much better to give it to us than leave it in
    the depot. If you leave it in the depot it'll either be pinched
    or they'll sell it. In any case you'll never see it again. You'll
    never see your underwear again.

WILLEM: If you leave it in the depot.

JOSEF K: Excuse me.

He goes into his room.

INT. K'S BEDROOM. DAY

K *opens a drawer in his desk, looks through papers, finds his bicycle
licence, which he puts aside, rummages until he finds his birth
certificate. He goes back into the sitting room.*

INT. K'S SITTING ROOM. DAY

As K *enters,* FRAU GRUBACH *is at the door of the sitting room leading
into the hall. She sees* K, *mutters 'Excuse me' and goes out.* K *looks
across to the window. The two men are sitting by it eating his
breakfast.*

JOSEF K: That's my breakfast.

WILLEM: Bloody good.

JOSEF K: These are my identity papers. I want to see yours. And I
    want to see the warrant for my arrest.

WILLEM: Oh good Christ, why do you keep trying to provoke us?
    Let me tell you something. We're probably the closest
    friends you've got in the world at this moment.

FRANZ: It's a fact.

JOSEF K: Here are my identity papers.

WILLEM *dips his bread and butter into a pot of honey.*

WILLEM: What do we want with those? Do you think you'll get this trial of yours over quicker by arguing with your warders about identity papers and warrants? We're just warders, don't you understand? We can't make head or tail of a legal document. We've got nothing to do with your case, except to guard you for as long as we're told and get paid for it. But we do know one thing. We know that the authorities would never order an arrest like this without very good grounds indeed. (*To* FRANZ) Right?

FRANZ: They don't make mistakes.

WILLEM: Oh no. They never go looking for crime, you see. They're just drawn to the guilty and then they send us out to make the arrest – which is according to the Law. That is the Law. So how could they make a mistake?

JOSEF K: I don't know this Law.

WILLEM: Well, that's so much the worse for you, isn't it?

FRANZ: (*To* WILLEM) Did you hear that? He admits he doesn't know the Law and at the same time he claims he's innocent.

WILLEM: You can't talk to some people.

K *walks away from them to the window. He looks out.*

WINDOW ACROSS THE STREET. DAY

The old woman is now standing with an even older man. She is clinging to him. They are both staring into the window of the sitting room.

INT. K'S SITTING ROOM. DAY

K *turns back to the men.*

JOSEF K: Take me to your Inspector.

WILLEM: When he tells us to, not before. Listen. Why don't you go to your room and sit there quietly? You're going to need all your strength, I can tell you that. But look, if you want to give us a little money we're perfectly happy to bring you some breakfast from the café down the street.

K *stands still. He looks at the men. He looks at the door leading to the hall. He looks back at the men.*

He turns, goes back into his bedroom.

INT. K'S BEDROOM. DAY
K takes off his nightshirt and quickly slips into a shirt. While doing this, he peers out of his window at the window across the street.

WINDOW ACROSS THE STREET. DAY
There is no one at the window.

INT. K'S BEDROOM. DAY
K tucks the shirt into his trousers. He picks up a green apple and bites into it. He puts the apple down carefully on the plate. He goes to a cupboard, takes out a bottle of brandy, pours a nip, drinks it, pours another, drinks it.
A shout from the next room.
WILLEM: The Inspector wants you!
JOSEF K: (*Shouting back*) At last!
 He goes into the sitting room.

INT. K'S SITTING ROOM. DAY
The two men stare at K, rush at him, push him back into his room.

INT. K'S BEDROOM. DAY
WILLEM: What do you think you're doing? Going to appear before the Inspector in your shirt? He'd have you flogged and us as well!
JOSEF K: Leave me alone! Stop pushing me.
WILLEM: Put on a jacket! Come on!
JOSEF K: Ridiculous!
 He takes a jacket out of his wardrobe.
FRANZ: Not that!
WILLEM: It has to be black.
JOSEF K: But it's not the official trial yet, is it?
WILLEM: It has to be black.
JOSEF K: Well, in that case I'll put on a black tie too.
 They watch K closely as he ties his black tie.
WILLEM: (*To* FRANZ) Go and tell the Inspector he's getting dressed.
 FRANZ *goes out.*
 K puts on his jacket, combs his hair, regards himself in the mirror. He turns.

He and WILLEM *go back into the sitting room.*

INT. K'S SITTING ROOM. DAY
WILLEM *leads* K *through the sitting room into Fräulein Bürstner's
room.*

INT. FRÄULEIN BÜRSTNER'S ROOM. DAY
Fräulein Bürstner's bedside table is in the middle of the room. The
INSPECTOR *is using it as a desk. He sits with his legs crossed.*
In a corner of the room three young men are standing looking at an
arrangement of snapshots on a mat hung up on a wall. The two
warders sit on a chest.
A white blouse is hanging on the catch of the open window.
Through the window, across the street, the old woman and the man are
staring into the room. Behind them stands a tall man, his shirt open at
the chest, squeezing a reddish pointed beard.
INSPECTOR: Josef K?
JOSEF K: Yes?
INSPECTOR: I suppose you're a bit surprised at what's happened
     this morning?
JOSEF K: I certainly am.
     The INSPECTOR *casually rearranges objects on the bedside table.*
     I certainly am surprised, but not very surprised.
INSPECTOR: You're not very surprised?
JOSEF K: I mean – Can I sit down?
INSPECTOR: It's not usual.
JOSEF K: I mean of course I'm surprised. But after all, the world
     is the world, one gets used to surprises, one doesn't take
     them too seriously, especially the kind of thing that's going
     on here today.
INSPECTOR: Oh? Why's that?
JOSEF K: I'm not going as far as to say that I look on the whole
     thing as a joke –
INSPECTOR: Quite right.
JOSEF K: But it's hardly to be taken seriously, is it? I mean I
     know I'm being charged – but with what and on what
     grounds and who is making the accusation? That is what I
     would like to know. This is a legally constituted state, the
     rule of law is fully established. Who are you? What is your

authority? I demand clear answers to these questions.

The INSPECTOR *throws a matchbox on to the table.*

INSPECTOR: You've really got it all wrong. We know nothing about your case. I don't even know whether you've been charged. You've just been arrested. That's all we know. But don't worry about us. Worry about yourself. Worry about what might happen to you. And don't talk so much.

K *stares at him. He then walks up and down the room.*

JOSEF K: I must phone a lawyer.

INSPECTOR: Phone who you like.

JOSEF K: I need a lawyer.

INSPECTOR: I don't see the point, quite frankly.

JOSEF K: You don't see the point of my calling a lawyer when I'm supposed to be under arrest? What the hell are you talking about?

INSPECTOR: No – all I meant was . . . I just don't see the point of calling a lawyer.

Pause.

JOSEF K: Well I won't then.

INSPECTOR: No no, do, if you feel like it. There's a phone in the hall. I saw it.

JOSEF K: No I won't. I don't want to.

K *goes to the window. The three people are still at the window opposite.*

K *opens the window, shouts across the street.*

Get away from that window!

The two old people hide behind the tall man.

(*To the* INSPECTOR) Look. Why don't we bring this matter to a close? Why don't we shake hands all round and call it a day? I don't see –

INSPECTOR: (*Standing*) Can't do that. Can't call it a day, I'm afraid.

He walks towards K.

Can't bring it to a close . . . just yet. But on the other hand I'm not saying you should give up hope. You're only under arrest, that's all. Well, we're off. You can go to work. You can go to your bank.

JOSEF K: Go to the bank? How can I go to the bank if I'm under arrest?

INSPECTOR: There's nothing to stop you going to the bank.

JOSEF K: Then this arrest isn't serious, as I said?

INSPECTOR: That's not for me to say. It's just an arrest. It's not for me to say how serious it is. That's for others. You don't have to go to the bank, of course. Do what you like. But I did arrange for these three colleagues of yours to be at your disposal to make your arrival at the bank as inconspicuous as possible.

K studies the three young men for the first time. They bow in turn.

RABENSTEINER: Rabensteiner.

KULLICH: Kullich.

KAMINER: Kaminer.

JOSEF K: Good morning. I didn't recognize you. What are you all doing here?

KAMINER giggles.

EXT. GRUBACH'S HOUSE. DAY

K and the three young men come out of the house. KAMINER runs to the corner to look for a taxi.
The tall man with the red beard comes out of the house opposite. He stops when he sees K and flattens himself against the wall. K glares at him.
KAMINER runs up with the taxi. They all get in.

INSIDE THE TAXI. DAY

Rabensteiner looking out of the right window. KULLICH looking out of the left. KAMINER sitting with a fixed grin.
K closes his eyes.

EXT. BANK. DAY

The taxi draws to a halt outside a large bank. K and the others get out and go into the bank.

INT. BANK: STAIRS AND MAIN HALL. DAY

RABENSTEINER, KULLICH and KAMINER follow K up the stairs and across the main mall. K stops, turns, glares at them. They stop still. K goes on towards the stairs at the rear of the hall.
He is greeted by various colleagues. He responds cheerfully.

INT. BANK: UPPER FLOOR. DAY

As K *reaches the landing, the* DEPUTY MANAGER *comes towards him, looking at his watch briefly. He greets* K *warmly, shakes his hand and puts his arm around* K's *shoulder.*

DEPUTY MANAGER: Just the man. We've had a very encouraging letter from . . .

    They walk away.

INT. BANK: K'S OFFICE. DAY

K *walking into his office. His* ASSISTANT *at the filing cabinet.*

K'S ASSISTANT: Happy birthday, sir.

JOSEF K: Thank you. Thank you very much.

    K *sits at his desk.*

K'S ASSISTANT: There are some presents for you, sir, from the staff.

JOSEF K: Oh, really? How nice of them.

    He looks at some wrapped packages on his desk, but does not open them. He opens a file and studies it.

INT. GRUBACH'S HOUSE: HER KITCHEN. NIGHT

FRAU GRUBACH *with a cake.*

FRAU GRUBACH: A little birthday cake. For my best and favourite lodger. I made it this afternoon.

JOSEF K: Very kind. But you shouldn't have done it. I've given you enough work today as it is.

FRAU GRUBACH: What work?

JOSEF K: I mean the men who were here this morning.

FRAU GRUBACH: They didn't give me any work.

    She cuts the cake and offers him a piece.

    There. Many happy returns of the day.

JOSEF K: (*Taking cake*) Well, it won't happen again.

FRAU GRUBACH: No, it can't happen again. Shall I join you? Shall I take a piece of cake?

JOSEF K: Yes of course, of course.

    They both eat.

FRAU GRUBACH: You mustn't take it to heart. Admitted you're under arrest, but it's not as if you're a thief or anything like that, is it?

JOSEF K: (*Smiling*) I'm not a thief, no. No no, I quite agree with

you. I don't think it matters in the least. I was just taken by
surprise, that's all. It could never have happened to me in the
bank, for example. I have my wits about me there. I'm
absolutely on top of things. But this morning I was simply
half asleep. Still, it's all over now. There's nothing more to
say about it. I just wanted your opinion, that's all. I'm glad
we agree. Now, let's shake hands on it and have done with it.
He extends his hand.
FRAU GRUBACH: Don't take it so hard, please, Herr K.
JOSEF K: I didn't know I was taking it hard.
FRAU GRUBACH: Have some more cake. You haven't said
    whether it's nice cake. Do you like the cake?
JOSEF K: It's extremely nice cake. Tell me. Is Fräulein Bürstner
    at home?
FRAU GRUBACH: No, she went to the theatre.
JOSEF K: I wanted to apologize to her for making use of her room
    today.
FRAU GRUBACH: But that isn't necessary. She knows nothing
    about it and it's all been tidied up anyway.
JOSEF K: Show me. Let me see.
    *She leads him to the door of Fräulein Bürstner's room. They go
    in.*

INT. FRÄULEIN BÜRSTNER'S ROOM. NIGHT
Moon in the room. High pillows on the bed.
FRAU GRUBACH: You see, you'd never know anyone had been in
    here at all, would you?
JOSEF K: She's often out late, isn't she?
FRAU GRUBACH: She's young.
JOSEF K: Mmnn.
FRAU GRUBACH: I don't want to say anything against her. But it's
    true that I've seen her twice this month in out-of-the-way
    streets and each time with a different man. I shall really have
    to speak to her about it.
JOSEF K: You've totally misunderstood me. I didn't mean
    anything like that. I warn you not to say anything to Fräulein
    Bürstner. I know her well. There's not a grain of truth in
    what you're implying. I warn you to say nothing to her.
    He stares at her.

Oh say what you like to her! Good night.

He moves to the door. She blocks his way.

FRAU GRUBACH: Oh Herr K, I just meant that it was in the interests of all the lodgers that I keep the house clean. That's all I meant.

JOSEF K: Clean! If you want to keep the house clean, you'll have to start by throwing me out!

INT. K'S SITTING ROOM AND HALL. NIGHT

K at the window looking down into the street.

He walks up and down the room. He opens his door a little, lies on the couch, lights a cigar, lies looking out into the hall.

He stubs out his cigar, closes his eyes.

He suddenly opens them.

FRÄULEIN BÜRSTNER, wearing a silk shawl over her dress, comes in the front door and goes towards her room. K goes to the crack in the door and whispers.

JOSEF K: Fräulein Bürstner.

She looks round.

FRÄULEIN BÜRSTNER: Yes?

JOSEF K: It's me.

He steps into the hall.

INT. GRUBACH'S HALL. NIGHT

FRÄULEIN BÜRSTNER: Herr K! Good evening.

She holds out her hand. He takes it.

JOSEF K: I've been waiting to have a word with you.

FRÄULEIN BÜRSTNER: A word?

JOSEF K: Yes.

FRÄULEIN BÜRSTNER: Now?

JOSEF K: Yes.

FRÄULEIN BÜRSTNER: Does it have to be now?

JOSEF K: I've been waiting for you since nine o'clock.

FRÄULEIN BÜRSTNER: It's just that I'm so tired I could drop. Well – if it must be now – come into my room for a minute. We can't talk here. There are people asleep.

They go into her room.

INT. FRÄULEIN BÜRSTNER'S ROOM. NIGHT

She puts a light on.

FRÄULEIN BÜRSTNER: Please sit down.

> *He does.*
>
> What is it?

JOSEF K: This morning your room was disarranged a little. It was disarranged by other people but it was partly my fault. I wanted to apologize to you.

> FRÄULEIN BÜRSTNER *looks about the room.*

FRÄULEIN BÜRSTNER: My room?

JOSEF K: That's right, yes. How it came about is not worth talking about.

FRÄULEIN BÜRSTNER: But surely that's the really interesting part? Isn't it?

JOSEF K: No. No it isn't.

FRÄULEIN BÜRSTNER: Well, I'm not going to . . . pry . . . so I can't see . . .

> *She walks about the room.*
>
> Nothing's been disturbed as far as I –
>
> *She stops at the wall of photographs.*
>
> Oh, no! Look. All my photos have been muddled up. What's been happening? Who did this?
>
> K *goes to her.*

JOSEF K: Not me. It wasn't me. I swear to you I didn't touch your photographs. The fact is the Commission of Enquiry brought along three bank clerks – one of them – I'll get him sacked as soon as possible – must have interfered with your photographs.

FRÄULEIN BÜRSTNER: A Commission of Enquiry?

JOSEF K: Yes. To see me.

FRÄULEIN BÜRSTNER: No? I don't believe it!

> *She laughs.*

JOSEF K: Why? Do you believe I'm innocent?

FRÄULEIN BÜRSTNER: Innocent? Innocent of what? Anyway I hardly know you. What I really meant was that you've got to be a pretty big criminal, haven't you, for them to set up a Commission of Enquiry. Isn't that right?

JOSEF K: I can see you don't know much about legal matters.

FRÄULEIN BÜRSTNER: No I don't. But guess what? I'm joining a law firm next month. I've always been attracted by the law.

JOSEF K: Really? Good. Well . . . perhaps you might be able to help me with my case.

FRÄULEIN BÜRSTNER: Why not?

JOSEF K: You see the thing's too petty for me to drag in a lawyer, but I might well need an adviser. Who knows?

FRÄULEIN BÜRSTNER: But if I'm to be your adviser I must know what it's all about.

JOSEF K: I don't know what it's about. I haven't been told what it's about.

FRÄULEIN BÜRSTNER: Is this a joke? (*She yawns.*) And it's so late! And I'm so tired.

JOSEF K: It wasn't actually a Commission of Enquiry at all. I only called it that because I couldn't think of a better name for it. There was no interrogation, you see. I was merely placed under arrest.

She laughs.

FRÄULEIN BÜRSTNER: What was it like?

JOSEF K: Horrible.

She is sitting on the settee. Her hand is slowly, abstractedly, caressing her hip. He watches this movement.

FRÄULEIN BÜRSTNER: That's too vague.

JOSEF K: Is it? Shall I show you what it was like then?

FRÄULEIN BÜRSTNER: I'm tired.

JOSEF K: You came in so late.

FRÄULEIN BÜRSTNER: I didn't know –

JOSEF K: The Inspector was sitting in the middle of this room – at your bedside table. The two warders sat on the chest. The three clerks stood by your photographs. A white blouse was hanging on that window. It still is. Look. A white blouse. I was awake. Wide awake. But the Inspector shouts at me as if I'm asleep, as if he's waking me up. He shouts: 'Josef K!'

The sound reverberates. There are knocks on the wall. She gasps. K grasps her hand. They whisper.

Don't be afraid. I'll sort everything out. But who's in there? There's no one sleeping there.

FRÄULEIN BÜRSTNER: There is! A nephew of Frau Grubach. A captain. I forgot about it myself. Oh why did you shout? Why did you have to shout?

JOSEF K: There's nothing to be worried about.
> *He takes her in his arms and kisses her.*

FRÄULEIN BÜRSTNER: Oh please go away, please, go on, go on,
he can hear everything.

JOSEF K: Come here.
> *He takes her to the far corner of the room.*

He can't hear us here. What's his name?

FRÄULEIN BÜRSTNER: His name? Oh . . . Lanz . . .

JOSEF K: Lanz . . . Lanz. I don't know him.

FRÄULEIN BÜRSTNER: Please –

JOSEF K: (*Taking her hand*) Listen. There's no danger. I promise
you. Frau Grubach adores me. I'm her favourite. I've also
lent her a substantial sum of money. Now listen. Listen to
me.

I'll agree to any explanation you suggest of how we came to
be together in your room, provided it's plausible. If you want
it spread around that I assaulted you then we'll tell Frau
Grubach precisely that and she'll believe it, she believes
everything I say.

FRÄULEIN BÜRSTNER *is staring at the ground.*

Why shouldn't she believe I assaulted you?

FRÄULEIN BÜRSTNER: The knocking frightened me, that's all. I
    take full responsibility for anything that happens in my
    room. Now please go. Please go.
JOSEF K: But you're not angry with me?
FRÄULEIN BÜRSTNER: No no, I'm never angry with anyone.
    She leads him to the door, slips out into the hall. She whispers.
    Come here. Look.

INT. GRUBACH'S HALL. NIGHT
K *joins her. She points to a light under a door.*
FRÄULEIN BÜRSTNER: He's listening.
    K *kisses her on the mouth, all over her face, her neck.*
    Good night.
    *He kisses her hand. She walks back to her room and closes the
    door. He stands.*

INT. BANK: K'S OFFICE. MORNING
K *at his desk.* K'S ASSISTANT *comes in the door.*
K'S ASSISTANT: The telephone for you, Herr K.
    K *stands and goes out of the room.*

INT. BANK: ANTE-ROOM. DAY
The telephone stands on a table. K *picks it up.*
JOSEF K: Good morning. Josef K.
VOICE: Josef K?
JOSEF K: Yes.
VOICE: There will be a first hearing of your case this coming
    Sunday.
JOSEF K: This Sunday?
VOICE: This coming Sunday.
JOSEF K: I see.
VOICE: We don't want to disturb your working week. So we
    assume Sunday suits you? But if not, do please say so.
    Hearings can be heard at night.
    K *says nothing.*
    Herr K?
JOSEF K: Yes?
VOICE: So we assume Sunday suits you?
JOSEF K: Yes, yes. Quite convenient.

VOICE: It is essential that you appear, of course. Absolutely
    obligatory.
JOSEF K: Yes, of course.
VOICE: So the date is agreed – which is this coming Sunday. The
    address is No. 48 Juliusstrasse.
JOSEF K: Juliusstrasse – ?
    The line goes dead. K stands still. He replaces the receiver. The
    DEPUTY MANAGER *is at his elbow.*
DEPUTY MANAGER: Bad news?
JOSEF K: No, no.
    The DEPUTY MANAGER *lifts the receiver and depresses the button*
    to call for the operator.
DEPUTY MANAGER: Oh, Herr K, would you like to join me on my
    yacht on Sunday? (*Into telephone*) Operator – yes – I would like
    Vienna 24046 please. (*To* K) A small party. The Public
    Prosecutor will be there. Do you know him? We would very
    much like you to come.
JOSEF K: I'm sorry. I'm afraid I have another engagement on
    Sunday.
DEPUTY MANAGER: Oh, what a pity. (*Into telephone*) Hello, hello?
    Yes. Herr Strauss. Good morning.
    The DEPUTY MANAGER *talks on.* K *stands still, frozen. The*
    DEPUTY MANAGER'*s voice is distant, muffled. He finally puts the*
    telephone down and looks at K *curiously.* K *turns sharply.*
JOSEF K: Someone just rang me up and asked me to go somewhere
    but they forgot to say the time.
DEPUTY MANAGER: Well, why don't you ring them back and ask?
JOSEF K: Oh, it's not that important.
    K *bows and walks back to his office.*

EXT. TRAMWAY. SUNDAY MORNING
K *walking. A tram passes.* K *suddenly sees* RABENSTEINER *and*
KULLICH (*two of the clerks*) *standing on the tram. They peer out at him.*

EXT. CAFÉ. DAY
K *walks on. He passes a café. On the terrace of the café he sees*
KAMINER (*the third clerk*). KAMINER *leans over the balustrade and*
gazes at K. K *walks on.*

EXT. JULIUSSTRASSE. DAY

A street of tenements. People at windows in shirtsleeves, some holding small children. Other windows piled high with bedding. People call to each other across the street. Laughter. Fruit vendors. A gramophone playing.

K finds No. 48. A barefooted man sitting on a case reading a newspaper. Boys playing. A girl in a dressing-gown pumping water into a can. Washing being stretched between two windows.

K goes through the gate into the yard. He looks at four flights of stairs, finally decides on one.

EXT. TENEMENT STAIRWAY. DAY

K climbs the stairs. On the first landing children playing with marbles. A marble rolls towards his feet. Two small boys hold on to K's trousers. He walks on. He stops at a door of a flat and knocks. The door opens. A WOMAN with a baby in her arms. Behind her a MAN in bed.

JOSEF K: Good morning.

WOMAN WITH BABY: Yes?

JOSEF K: I'm looking . . .

    He stops, is blank.

WOMAN WITH BABY: Yes? What is it?

JOSEF K: I'm . . . I'm looking for a plumber . . .

WOMAN WITH BABY: A plumber?

JOSEF K: Called Lanz.

MAN IN BED: What does he want?

WOMAN WITH BABY: He's looking for a plumber called Lanz.

MAN IN BED: Shut the door.

    She does.

    K walks up the next flight of stairs.

EXT. TENEMENT STAIRWAY: NEXT LANDING. DAY

K knocks on a door. There is no answer. A door two flats along opens. A man looks out.

FIRST STAIRMAN: Yes? What is it?

JOSEF K: I'm looking for a plumber called Lanz.

FIRST STAIRMAN: A plumber called Lanz?

JOSEF K: Yes.

FIRST STAIRMAN: Lanz, Lanz. You're sure his name is Lanz?

    No, I'll tell you what, there is a plumber upstairs, at least I

think he's a plumber, I mean that's what he says he is, but I wouldn't swear his name was Lanz, I mean if I had to swear it on oath, I wouldn't swear it.

Another MAN *appears.*

SECOND STAIRMAN: What's the trouble?

FIRST STAIRMAN: This man is looking for a man called Lanz. He says he's a plumber.

SECOND STAIRMAN: Who is?

JOSEF K: Lanz.

SECOND STAIRMAN: Ah. Lanz, yes. Yes yes, there used to be a man called Lanz on the fifth floor. That's right. I remember. He was a plumber. Definitely. But I haven't been up there for years.

JOSEF K: On the fifth floor?

SECOND STAIRMAN: I've got no reason to go up there now, you see.

JOSEF K: Thank you.

EXT. TENEMENT STAIRWAY: TOP FLOOR. DAY

K *walks to the door, knocks, turns the handle and goes in.*

INT. TENEMENT: WASHERWOMAN'S FLAT. DAY

The room is quite bare. A young WOMAN *is washing clothes in a tub. A clock on the wall says ten o'clock.*

JOSEF K: I'm looking for a plumber called Lanz.

WASHERWOMAN: Yes. (*She points to an inner door.*) In there.
   K *goes to the door and opens it.*

INT. THE COURTROOM. DAY

The room is packed. There is a low dais at the end of the room. A small fat man sits at a table, laughing with another. Everyone is talking. K *goes back into the first room.*

INT. TENEMENT: WASHERWOMAN'S FLAT. DAY

K *goes to the woman at the tub.*

JOSEF K: I said I was looking for a plumber, a man called Lanz.

WASHERMAN: Yes, that's right. In there. I told you. Go in there. You're very late anyway.
   She goes to the door. He follows.
   I've got to shut the door after you. No one else is allowed in.
   She opens the door. He stares into the room.
   Come on.
   He goes in. She closes the door.

INT. THE COURTROOM. DAY

There is still a great deal of noise. Nobody looks at K. *He stands.*

Someone touches his hand. He looks down. It is a small BOY. K *takes the* BOY's *hand. The* BOY *leads him through the crowd to the dais. The fat man (the* EXAMINING MAGISTRATE) *is still laughing and whispering with another man. The* BOY *stands on tiptoe, touches the* MAGISTRATE's *arm. The* MAGISTRATE *looks down. The* BOY *mutters. The* MAGISTRATE *looks at* K. *He takes out a watch, glances at it, looks back at* K.

MAGISTRATE: You should have been here an hour and five minutes ago.

People in the room turn to look at the dais. A murmur grows.

You should have been here an hour and five minutes ago.

The murmur grows and then dies away. The room becomes quiet.

JOSEF K: I may be late, but at least I've come.

A burst of applause from the room.

MAGISTRATE: Yes, but I'm no longer obliged to hear you. However, I'm willing to make an exception in this case. Step up.

K *gets on to the dais. The* MAGISTRATE *picks up a small, dirty notebook. He looks through it.*

You are a house painter.

JOSEF K: No, I am senior clerk in a large bank.

A burst of laughter from the room. People rest their hands on their knees and shake with laughter. K *joins in. The* MAGISTRATE *jumps up and glares at the room.*

Your question, Mr Examining Magistrate, as to whether I am a house painter – although it wasn't a question but a statement – demonstrates the kind of proceedings that are being instituted against me. You may argue that they are not legal proceedings at all, and you would be right, for they are in fact only legal proceedings if I recognize them as such. Well, for the moment I choose to recognize them, but only out of a kind of pity.

K *stops. There is absolute silence in the room, a tense attention. The* MAGISTRATE *remains standing.*

The door opens. The WASHERWOMAN *comes in. People turn to look at her. She stands at the back wall. The* MAGISTRATE *sits and picks up the notebook.* K *snatches the notebook from him and holds it up with two fingers, wrinkling his nose. He waves it about.*

There are the Court records! Look at this miserable smelly grimy little book! Pathetic!

He drops it on the table.
What has happened to me, ladies and gentleman, is only an isolated incident and of little importance. But it is an indication of the kind of intimidation many people are being subjected to. It is for these people I am speaking – not for myself.

VOICES: Bravo! Bravo! And bravo again!

JOSEF K: I was arrested ten days ago. Those who arrested me were at the very best degenerate, arrogant, ignorant and corrupt. Their every action declared this. They ate my breakfast, they even tried to steal my underwear. Such an arrest is exactly the same as being waylaid by a bunch of louts in a dark alley. No more, no less. The dignity of the law – what a joke! They chain-ganged three junior clerks from my bank as witnesses, in order, obviously, to damage my public reputation and undermine my position at the bank. I want to remind you that I am quite detached from this whole business and so am able to judge it calmly.
Silence.
There is no doubt that behind all the outward manifestations of this tribunal's authority there exists a huge organization. An organization which not only employs corrupt warders, stupid inspectors, totally incompetent examining magistrates, but which also makes use of a judicial network of senior officials with a vast and indispensable retinue of servants, clerks, policemen and other auxiliaries – perhaps even hangmen – no I'm not afraid to use that word. And what is the significance of this great organization? I'll tell you. It consists of securing the arrest of innocent people and instituting against them senseless proceedings that usually – as in my case – lead to nothing.
A scream from the back of the room.
A MAN *is pressing the* WASHERWOMAN *into a corner. Her blouse is off. People jump up and crowd around them.*
Stop that! Throw them out! Order! Order!
K *glares at the* MAGISTRATE, *who is sitting calmly at his table.*
I'll throw them out myself.
K *jumps down from the dais. He tries to get through the crowd. He is barred, prevented. People grapple with him, grab him.*

He fights his way through and gets to the door. The
WASHERWOMAN *is on the floor, the* MAN *on top of her.*
A sudden silence. The EXAMINING MAGISTRATE *is at the door*
of the room.

MAGISTRATE: It is my duty to point out to you that you have
today thrown away all the advantages that a hearing can
afford an arrested man.

JOSEF K: To hell with your damn hearings!
He opens the door, goes through it and slams it.

INT. BANK: THE MAIN HALL. MORNING
K *walking through the hall. Various men wish him good morning and*
shake his hand.

INT. BANK: ANTE-ROOM. DAY
He walks into the ante-room. The telephone is ringing. His
ASSISTANT *takes it.*

K'S ASSISTANT: For you, Herr K. Paris branch.

JOSEF K: I'll call back later.

K'S ASSISTANT: But it's Monsieur Schrader himself.

JOSEF K: I'll call back later.

K walks towards his office. In background the ASSISTANT *speaks into the phone.*

K'S ASSISTANT: Herr K is extremely sorry but he's unable to come to the telephone at this precise moment . . .

INT. BANK: K'S OFFICE. DAY

K *at his desk examining files. The* ASSISTANT *comes in.*

JOSEF K: Have there been any telephone messages for me this morning?

K'S ASSISTANT: Telephone messages?

JOSEF K: Yes.

K'S ASSISTANT: Well, Monsieur Schrader from Paris –

JOSEF K: No, no. Apart from that.

K'S ASSISTANT: I'm sorry Herr K . . . Who from?

JOSEF K: Who from? From anybody!

    Pause.

K'S ASSISTANT: No, sir.

INT. GRUBACH'S HOUSE: HALL. NIGHT

K *comes through the front door into the hall.* FRAU GRUBACH *comes out of her room.*

FRAU GRUBACH: Herr K –

JOSEF K: Have there been any telephone messages for me?

FRAU GRUBACH: No, no, none. Herr K, I'm worried about you. Are you eating? I don't think you're eating.

JOSEF K: I asked you if anyone had left a message for me on the telephone.

FRAU GRUBACH: I'm sorry . . . what kind of message?

JOSEF K: What kind? Any kind. It doesn't matter what kind. It's a simple question. I would be grateful if you would answer it simply.

FRAU GRUBACH: But Herr K . . . the telephone hasn't rung at all today.

JOSEF K: How do you know? Weren't you out shopping this morning?

FRAU GRUBACH: Yes. Yes . . .

JOSEF K: So how can you know it hasn't rung? How can you *know?*

    She stares at him.

I really don't know why we're having this conversation.
Good night.
He goes to his room.

INT. K'S SITTING ROOM. NIGHT
*K at his desk feverishly writing a letter. He puts it in an envelope,
addresses the envelope to Fräulein Bürstner, goes out.*

INT. GRUBACH'S HOUSE: THE HALL. NIGHT
K sliding the envelope under Fräulein Bürstner's door.

EXT. JULIUSSTRASSE. SUNDAY MORNING
K walking towards the house.

INT. TENEMENT STAIRWAY. DAY
K climbing the stairs. A third man appears.
THIRD STAIRMAN: Oh, hello sir. Good morning to you. Tell me,
    did you find the plumber Lanz?
JOSEF K: The plumber Lanz? Yes I did. Yes. I found him.
THIRD STAIRMAN: So he's still here after all these years, eh? (*He
    shakes his head.*) After all these years!
JOSEF K: Good morning.
    K climbs the next flight of stairs.

EXT. TENEMENT STAIRWAY: TOP FLOOR. DAY
K knocks on the door. The woman opens it.
JOSEF K: Good morning.

INT. WASHERWOMAN'S FLAT/COURTROOM. DAY
He walks through the room to the other door.
WASHERWOMAN: There's no session today.
JOSEF K: No session?
    *She goes to the door and opens it. They look in. The room is
    empty.*
JOSEF K: You're right. There's no session. Why didn't they tell
    me? How can they expect me to know? What are those books
    on the table?
WASHERWOMAN: They belong to the Examining Magistrate.
    You're not allowed to touch them.

She closes the door.
Do you want me to give any message to the Examining Magistrate?
JOSEF K: Do you know him?
WASHERWOMAN: Of course I know him. My husband is the Court Usher.
K looks about the room. It is fully furnished.
JOSEF K: Last Sunday there was just a washtub in here.
WASHERWOMAN: We have to clear everything out of the room on days when the Court is in session. It's so tiring. Listen. I'm sorry I caused a disturbance in the middle of your speech. It wasn't my fault. That man never leaves me alone, he's wild about me, he can't keep his hands off me. There's nothing I can do to stop it. Even my husband has come to accept it. If he wants to keep his job he's got to put up with it – the man is a law student, you see – they say he's going to be really powerful some day. But it was a pity he disturbed your speech. I was really enjoying it. Of course I only heard part of it. I missed the beginning and during the last bit I was on the floor with the law student. But I was really impressed. I thought to myself – I only wish there was a way I could help him.
JOSEF K: There is.
WASHERWOMAN: How?
JOSEF K: Let me examine those books in the other room.
She looks at him and opens the door. They go in.

INT. EMPTY COURTROOM. DAY
K and the WASHERWOMAN *go to the table.*
JOSEF K: God this place is filthy.
The WASHERWOMAN *picks up the books and wipes them with her apron.* K *takes one from her and opens it.*
Obscene photographs! Ha!
He opens another.
More.
He opens another.
And more. And more.
He throws the books down.
So these are the law books that are studied here. These are

the kind of men who are supposed to be judging me.

WASHERWOMAN: I'll help you. Let me help you. Come. Sit down
with me.

They sit.

You've got lovely dark eyes. Haven't you? Such lovely dark
eyes.

JOSEF K: I don't see how you can help me. To help me you'd have
to know the senior officials well. You only know that fat lout
the Examining Magistrate. He's hardly a senior official.

WASHERWOMAN: Well, he may be a minor official but I can tell
you he never stops writing reports, especially about you.
Last Sunday he stayed up writing till all hours. I woke up in
the middle of the night and he was looking down at me (my
husband was fast asleep) and he whispered to me that he
would never forget the sight of me in my nightie in bed. So
you see he really fancies me – so I can influence him. And
guess what he sent me yesterday? These lovely silk
stockings. Look.

She lifts her skirt.

Aren't they lovely stockings? Can you believe that an
Examining Magistrate would give such beautiful stockings to
a woman like me? Sshh. Berthold is watching us.

K *looks up.* BERTHOLD, *the student, is standing in the doorway.*
Listen, don't be angry with me, but I've got to go to him,
he's a disgusting man, I can't bear him, just look at his bandy
legs, but I've got to go to him. But I'll come back. Then I'll
go with you wherever you like and you can do whatever you
like with me.

She goes to the STUDENT. *He puts his arms around her, presses
his body against her, whispers.*

K *raps on the table.*

The STUDENT *kisses her mouth and throat.*

K *bangs on the table with his fist.*

The STUDENT *feels her body.*

K *stands and stamps around the room.*

BERTHOLD: Why don't you get out of here?

JOSEF K: Not me, sir. You.

BERTHOLD: (*To* WASHERWOMAN) They've given him too much
leeway. He should have been confined to his room. I've been

trying to tell the Examining Magistrate but it's like talking to a brick wall.

K goes towards them. He holds out his hand to the WOMAN.

JOSEF K: Come here.

BERTHOLD: Oh no.

The STUDENT *picks the* WOMAN *up and runs to the door of the flat. The* WOMAN *calls to* K.

WASHERWOMAN: It's no good, the Examining Magistrate has sent for me, this little monster won't let me go –

K follows them.

JOSEF K: I'll save you.

WASHERWOMAN: No, no you mustn't! It would be the end of me. He's just carrying out the orders of the court. Leave us alone. Please!

JOSEF K: Yes! I'll leave you alone! I never want to see you again!

The STUDENT *carries the* WOMAN *out of the flat, followed slowly by* K.

EXT. TENEMENT STAIRWAY: TOP FLOOR. DAY

The STUDENT *carries the* WOMAN *up a narrow wooden staircase. She waves down to* K *and shrugs helplessly.*

K suddenly notices a piece of cardboard near the stairs. On it is written in childish handwriting COURT OFFICES UPSTAIRS.

The USHER *comes up the stairs. He looks through the open door into the flat and turns to* K.

USHER: Have you seen a woman around here? My wife?

JOSEF K: You're the Court Usher.

USHER: Yes. And I know you. I recognize you. You were here last Sunday. Right? You're defendant K.

The USHER *offers his hand.* K *takes it. They shake hands.*

JOSEF K: I was speaking to your wife a short while ago. The student has taken her off to the Examining Magistrate.

USHER: You know, if I didn't depend on them so much I'd have squashed that student on the wall ages ago. Here, next to the notice. I'm always dreaming of doing it. I think of him right here, just here, a little above the floor, his arms outstretched, do you follow? His fingers spread out, his bandy legs twitching, blood all over the place, total agony, do you know what I mean? Unfortunately so far it's only a dream.

K *smiles.*

JOSEF K: I understand your feelings.

USHER: And now it's gone from bad to worse. Before, he only took her to his own place, but now he's taking her to the Examining Magistrate as well. It's pretty humiliating, I can tell you. And there's bugger-all I can do about it.

JOSEF K: No, I see that.

USHER: But you could do something about it. You could give that student such a hiding, if you felt like it, that he might really think twice before he touched her up again. But only a man like you could do it.

JOSEF K: A man like me? Why?

USHER: Because you're an accused man. You've got nothing to lose.

K *is silent.*

Perhaps you could think about it.

K *is silent.*

Well, I've got to report to the Court offices. You want to come and have a look?

JOSEF K: A look?

USHER: At the offices. No one'll notice. I just thought you might be interested.

JOSEF K: Oh. Yes. Why not?

He follows the USHER *up the stairs. The* USHER *opens the door at the top. They go in.*

INT. THE COURT OFFICES. DAY

A corridor. Two rows of long wooden benches. People sitting on the benches. As K *and the* USHER *pass, they stand.*

JOSEF K: What are they standing for?

USHER: They're all defendants.

JOSEF K: Yes, but why are they standing? Who do they think I am? It's idiotic.

K *stops by a tall thin man.*

What are you doing here? Why are you waiting here?

The man does not reply.

USHER: Come on, sir. The gentleman is only asking you what you're waiting for. Answer him.

THIN DEFENDANT: I'm waiting . . .

Men collect around them.

USHER: Move out of it. Don't block the corridor.

They withdraw.

JOSEF K: I asked you what you were doing here.

THIN DEFENDANT: A month ago I offered some evidence to the Court concerning my case. I am now waiting for the Court's view of it. I am waiting for the Court's view of my evidence.

JOSEF K: You're waiting for the Court's view?

THIN DEFENDANT: That's right. Precisely. I'm waiting for the Court's view.

JOSEF K: Well, let me tell you, I am also a defendant, but you'll have to wait a very long time before I 'offer evidence' to this Court. I can assure you of that. A very long time. I wouldn't demean myself. And I am also an accused man. Do you understand me?

The man stares at him.

THIN DEFENDANT: I have offered evidence . . .

JOSEF K: What are you saying? Are you saying that you don't believe that I'm also a defendant? That I'm also an accused man?

THIN DEFENDANT: Oh yes, yes –

JOSEF K: No, tell me the truth. Are you saying you don't believe me? Are you saying you don't believe I'm an accused man? What are you saying? Speak up. Are you saying you don't believe me?

He grasps the man's shoulders and shakes him violently. The man screams. K pushes him back on to his bench. K and the USHER walk on.

USHER: They're very sensitive, some of these defendants.

In the background a group collects around the man who screamed. K and the USHER walk on.

JOSEF K: I think I'll go now.

USHER: But you haven't seen everything yet.

JOSEF K: I don't want to see everything. Actually I'm tired. I feel tired. Which is the way out?

USHER: Well . . . just go as far as the corner – turn right – then straight down the corridor until you reach the door.

JOSEF K: Can you show me the way? Please.

USHER: What do you mean? There's only one way. I just told you the way. Anyway I've got to deliver a message.

JOSEF K: Come with me! Show me!

USHER: Don't shout! Stop all that shouting.

JOSEF K: Come with me. Show me. Come with me.

> K *suddenly staggers and falls on the* USHER, *who catches him. The* USHER *holds on to* K, *turns him round and runs him down the corridor to the door.*
> *A sudden flash of light, a draught of fresh air. The* USHER's *voice – distant – then suddenly louder.*

USHER: First he wants to go and then when you tell him a hundred times that this is the exit, he won't move.

> *The door is open.* K *falls out, sits, gasps, takes in the air. The* USHER *slams the door.*

EXT. TENEMENT STAIRWAY. DAY

K *blinks, picks up his hat and bounds down the stairs.*

INT. K'S BEDROOM. DAY

K *sitting still. A knock on the door.* FRAU GRUBACH's *voice.*

FRAU GRUBACH: Herr K?

> *He looks at the door.*
> Herr K?

JOSEF K: Yes.

FRAU GRUBACH: Fräulein Montag would be grateful if she could have a word with you in the dining room.

> K *stands and looks at the door. Silence.*
> *He opens the door. The sitting room is empty.*
> *He goes into the hall.*

INT. GRUBACH'S HALL. DAY

The hall is empty. K *goes into the dining room.*

INT. GRUBACH'S DINING ROOM. DAY

FRÄULEIN MONTAG *is standing by the window.* K *closes the door. A long dining table is set for lunch.*

FRÄULEIN MONTAG: I don't know whether you know me.

JOSEF K: Of course. You have a room here. You've been living here for quite a long time.

FRÄULEIN MONTAG: But we've never spoken.

JOSEF K: No.

FRÄULEIN MONTAG: Would you mind if I had a few words with
you now?

K *is silent.*

It's on behalf of my friend, Fräulein Bürstner.

K *is silent.*

I shall be sharing her room with her from tomorrow, at her
invitation. We are friends. She hopes you will listen to me
for a minute, no more.

K *is silent.*

Over the last few weeks you have written a number of
letters to Fräulein Bürstner asking for a talk with her. She
knows what this talk would be about and is convinced that
it would be in neither her interest nor yours for such a talk
to take place. She thinks it would be pointless. I
volunteered to let you know this as I am quite uninvolved
and know nothing about the matter. That is all I have to
say.

JOSEF K: I am grateful to you.

K goes to the door. As he reaches it, it opens. CAPTAIN LANZ
comes in. He ignores K.

CAPTAIN LANZ: Fräulein Montag.

He goes to her, bows, kisses her hand.

FRÄULEIN MONTAG: Captain Lanz. Good morning.

K leaves the room.

INT. GRUBACH'S HALL. DAY

*K goes to Fräulein Bürstner's room, knocks. He knocks again. He
opens the door and looks in.*

INT. FRÄULEIN BÜRSTNER'S ROOM. DAY

The room is empty.

*K looks about the room. There is a second bed. The wardrobes are
open. Women's dresses, underwear, etc., lie all over the room. He
closes the door.*

INT. GRUBACH'S HALL. DAY

In the doorway of the dining room FRÄULEIN MONTAG *and*
CAPTAIN LANZ *are talking quietly.*

INT. BANK. K'S OFFICE AND ANTE-ROOM. EVENING
*K packing up his desk. He switches off the lights. In a far office lights
are on and figures move.*

INT. BANK: BACK CORRIDOR. NIGHT
*K walks down the corridor, stops.
He hears moaning.
He listens, turns to look at the lumber-room door.
Moaning.
He goes to the door and opens it.*

INT. BANK: THE LUMBER ROOM. NIGHT
*A candle on a shelf. Three men are in the room: the two WARDERS
and the FLOGGER.*
FRANZ: Sir! We're going to be flogged! Look! We're going to be
    flogged because you complained about us to the Examining
    Magistrate!
JOSEF K: I didn't complain. I just gave him my views.
WILLEM: But sir, if you only knew how badly we were paid you
    wouldn't be so hard on us. I have a family to feed, Franz
    wants to get married –
JOSEF K: But I never asked for you to be punished. I promise
    you. I was only concerned with the principle of the thing.
THE FLOGGER: The punishment is well deserved.
WILLLEM: Don't listen to him.
    The FLOGGER hits him with his birch. WILLEM cries out.
    (*To K*) This is a terrible tragedy, can't you see that? We're
    professionals, we've never fallen down on a job, we had every
    prospect of promotion, we would have become floggers like
    him and now look at us!
    K turns to the FLOGGER.
JOSEF K: Can we perhaps discuss this? Is there any chance of – ?
THE FLOGGER: There's no chance. (*To the two men*) Get your
    shirts off! Strip! (*To K*) They're talking rubbish. Do you
    think they would ever have made him a flogger? Don't be
    ridiculous. Look how fat he is. Do you know how he got so

fat? He eats the breakfasts of all those he arrests. He ate your
breakfast too, didn't he? I'll tell you something. No man
with a belly like that stands a chance of becoming a flogger.
It's out of the question.

WILLEM: It's not true!

THE FLOGGER: Shut up!

He hits him with his birch. K *takes out his wallet.*

JOSEF K: If you let them go, we could come to an arrangement.

THE FLOGGER: You want to get me flogged as well, do you? No
thanks.

JOSEF K: Listen. They're blameless. Honestly. It's the
organization that's to blame. It's the high officials who are to
blame.

BOTH WARDERS: That's right!

The FLOGGER *hits them.* K *pushes the birch down.*

JOSEF K: If you were birching one of the senior judges – believe
me – I would be right behind you.

THE FLOGGER: It's my job to flog people I'm told to flog and
that's what I'm going to do.

FRANZ *falls on his knees in front of* K.

FRANZ: Please. Get me off. He's older than me, he's not as
sensitive as me. I'm sensitive. I'm in love with my fiancée.
Please.

He weeps.

THE FLOGGER: I'm not waiting any longer.

He whips FRANZ'*s back savagely.* FRANZ *screams.*

The scream is unending.

JOSEF K: Don't scream!

FRANZ *lurches towards him.* K *pushes him back. He falls over.*

The FLOGGER *follows him, hitting him.*

INT. BANK: BACK CORRIDOR. NIGHT

K *looks up the corridor. Two* CLERKS *are approaching, curiously.*

K *shuts the door, goes to a window in the corridor and looks down. He*
calls to the two men.

JOSEF K: It's all right! It's me – the senior clerk.

CLERK: Is everything all right?

JOSEF K: There was a dog howling in the yard.

They stand uncertainly.

You can get back to your work.
The CLERKS *walk away.*
K *looks at the lumber-room door. He goes to it and listens.*
Absolute silence.

EXT. CITY STEPS. NIGHT
Crowds of people climbing and descending the steps. K *standing quite*
still at the centre of the activity.

INT. THE BANK. K'S OFFICE. MORNING
K *at his desk. He is dictating a letter to his* ASSISTANT. *He stops in*
mid-sentence, falls silent. The ASSISTANT *sits, pencil poised, finally*
looks at him.
K'S ASSISTANT: Herr K?
JOSEF K: I need to consult my files. Will you come back in an hour?
K'S ASSISTANT: Yes, Herr K.
  K *sits still. Over this the sounds of hundreds of voices in the bank,*
  filing cabinets opening, closing, echoing, etc.

INT. BANK: BACK CORRIDOR. LATE AFTERNOON
The lumber-room door.
The corridor is silent, empty.
K *appears at the top of the corridor. He walks slowly down it to the*
lumber-room door.
Silence.
He opens the door.

INT. BANK: LUMBER ROOM. LATE AFTERNOON
The FLOGGER *flogging the* WARDERS. *The* WARDERS *turn to the door.*
WARDERS: Sir! Sir!
  K *slams the door.*

INT. BANK: BACK CORRIDOR. LATE AFTERNOON
K *turns up the corridor. Three young* CLERKS *come round the corner.*
K *runs into them. He shouts at them.*
JOSEF K: It's time you cleared out that lumber room! We're going
  to be smothered in filth!
  K *walks fast in the direction of his office.*

INT. BANK: K'S OFFICE. LATE AFTERNOON
K comes in and sits at his desk. His ASSISTANT *follows with documents.*

K'S ASSISTANT: I've been through the Amsterdam documents, Herr K. They're ready for your signature.

JOSEF K: Are they in order?

K'S ASSISTANT: Absolutely in order, sir.

JOSEF K: Good, good. (*Looks at the page.*) Let me see . . .

K'S ASSISTANT: Here, sir.

He signs. The ASSISTANT *gives him another page.*
And here, sir, if you would be so kind.
K *signs.*
The door bursts open. K'S UNCLE *comes in.*

K'S UNCLE: Josef!

JOSEF K: Uncle! What a –

K'S UNCLE: Is it true? Tell me. Is it true?

JOSEF K: (*To* ASSISTANT) Excuse me please.

K'S UNCLE: Is it true? I'm asking you.

The ASSISTANT *goes out.*

JOSEF K: Sit down, Uncle.

K'S UNCLE: (*Sitting*) I'm asking you if it's true?

JOSEF K: I wish I knew what you were talking about.

K'S UNCLE: I am your guardian. Your welfare is of the utmost importance to me. You know that.
K *glances absently out of the window.*

K'S UNCLE: You're looking out of the window!

JOSEF K: Oh I'm sorry – what – ?
They stare at each other.
Oh, I suppose you've heard something about my trial.

K'S UNCLE: Yes, I've heard about your trial. But just that there's a case against you – not what it is. So it is true?

JOSEF K: Mmnn. Yes, it is.

K'S UNCLE: But what sort of case is it? Surely not a criminal case?

JOSEF K: Yes. A criminal case.

K'S UNCLE: And you can just sit there calmly with a criminal case hanging over your head?

JOSEF K: The calmer I am the more chance I have.

K'S UNCLE: Just tell me what it's all about! Is it something to do with the bank?

JOSEF K: No, it isn't. But, Uncle, you're talking too loudly. We'd
    better go out. Come on.
    They go to the door and out. K *has a brief word with his*
    ASSISTANT.

INT. BANK: MAIN HALL. DUSK
The DEPUTY MANAGER *and other officials are standing in the hall
talking.* K *and* UNCLE *walk towards the main exit.*
K'S UNCLE: But what kind of trial is it? I just don't understand!
    The officials glance at K. K *takes* UNCLE's *elbow and laughs.*

INT. BANK: STAIRS. DUSK
They go down the steps towards the street.
JOSEF K: Now I can speak.
K'S UNCLE: Speak.
JOSEF K: First of all, Uncle, this is not a case which will be heard
    by an ordinary court.
K'S UNCLE: That's bad.
JOSEF K: Why?
K'S UNCLE: It's bad.
JOSEF K: It's not something you should take too seriously, you
    know.

EXT. BANK: DUSK
K'S UNCLE: Josef! You used to be intelligent! Have you gone
    mad? Do you know what it will mean if such a case goes
    against you? You'll be wiped out. Wiped out! Finished.
    He hails a passing taxi.
    Jump in. Jump in.
    He gives the driver an address.

INT. TAXI. NIGHT
K'S UNCLE: We're going to Huld, the lawyer. He was at school
    with me. He's a great lawyer, a great lawyer.
JOSEF K: Oh. But does he know anything about cases . . . like
    mine?
K'S UNCLE: He knows. Yes.

EXT. DR HULD'S HOUSE. NIGHT
The taxi stops by a dark house.

EXT. DR HULD'S FRONT DOOR. NIGHT
UNCLE *rings the bell.*
Black eyes appear at a peephole.
K'S UNCLE: Open up! I'm a friend of the lawyer's.
    LENI *opens the door. They go in.*

INT. HULD'S HALL. NIGHT
LENI: Dr Huld is ill.
K'S UNCLE: What is it? His heart?
LENI: I think so.
    Holding a candle, she leads them to the bedroom.

INT. HULD'S BEDROOM. NIGHT
DR HULD *is in bed. The room is full of shadows.*
HULD: Who is it, Leni?
K'S UNCLE: It's your old friend Albert.
HULD: Ah, Albert.
    He slumps back.
K'S UNCLE: Not too good, eh?
HULD: I'm weaker every day.
    LENI *goes to the bed, arranges his pillows, whispers to him.* K
    watches her. She is aware of his gaze.
    UNCLE *paces up and down.*
K'S UNCLE: (*To* LENI) Please leave us alone. I have some personal
    business to discuss with my friend.
LENI: Dr Huld is ill. He isn't able to discuss any business.
K'S UNCLE: You damned impertinent bitch!
HULD: Leni's a good girl. She looks after me. You can say
    anything in front of her.
K'S UNCLE: But this isn't my business. It's somebody else's
    business.
HULD: Whose?
K'S UNCLE: My nephew. I brought him along with me.
    UNCLE *brings* K *forward.*
Josef K. Senior clerk.
    HULD *leans out of the bed. He takes* K's *hand.*

HULD: Forgive me, I didn't see you. All right, Leni, you can go.
    She goes. HULD *sits up.*
    So you've come to see me on business. That's a different
    matter.
K'S UNCLE: You look better already.
HULD: Let me say at once that your nephew's case interests me so
    much that – while my heart is not good – if he wished me to
    act on his behalf I would be unable to resist such a challenge.
JOSEF K: I don't understand –
HULD: Have *I* misunderstood? I thought you wanted to talk to me
    about your trial?
K'S UNCLE: Of course he did! That's why we're here. (*To* K)
    What do you mean, you don't understand?
JOSEF K: (*To* HULD) I would like to know how on earth you can
    possibly know anything about me and my trial.
HULD: Ah, I see. Well, I am a lawyer, I move in legal circles.
    People talk about different cases and one remembers the
    more striking ones. Especially if the nephew of a friend is
    involved. There's nothing remarkable in that, surely?
JOSEF K: You move . . . in those circles?
HULD: Of course.
K'S UNCLE: Really! You're talking like a child.
JOSEF K: (*To* HULD) And you say they are discussing my case in
    these circles?
HULD: It has certainly been referred to. You see, my moving in
    these circles is of great advantage to my clients in many ways.
    My illness restricts me of course – but I do receive visits from
    good friends of mine from the Court who keep me
    wonderfully well informed. There's a great friend of mine
    here in this room at this very moment, as a matter of fact.
    He points to a dark corner. K *turns. A* MAN *is sitting in the
    shadows. He stands, walks slowly into the light.*
    This is my friend Albert K. This is his nephew Josef K and
    this is the Chief Clerk of the court.
    All murmur 'How do you do?'
    I must say that it seems to me that we might take advantage
    of the Chief Clerk's presence to ask his advice in the matter
    of your case.
K'S UNCLE: A heaven-sent opportunity! Heaven sent.

CHIEF CLERK: If I can be of any assistance . . . I shall be only
     too . . .
HULD: Splendid. Let us draw up chairs –
     A sound of smashing china from somewhere in the apartment.
     They all turn.
JOSEF K: I'll see what's going on.
     He goes out.

INT. HULD'S HOUSE: DARK CORRIDOR. NIGHT
K *peering. A hand slides into his.* LENI *whispers.*
LENI: It's all right. I just threw a plate against the wall to bring
     you out.
JOSEF K: Oh.
LENI: Come here.
     She leads him to a room, opens the door.
     In here.
     They go in.

INT. HULD'S STUDY. NIGHT
LENI *takes him to sit on a large chest.*
LENI: I thought you would come to me without me having to get
     you out. You couldn't keep your eyes off me in the bedroom,
     could you? And yet you kept me waiting.
JOSEF K: I had to listen to the old men rambling on, I couldn't
     just run off without an excuse.
LENI: The fact is you didn't like me and you probably still don't
     like me even now. Do you want to know what my name is?
JOSEF K: What is it?
LENI: It's Leni.
     She takes his hand.
     Call me Leni.
     K *stares at her blankly.*
     Can't you think of anything else except your trial?
JOSEF K: I'm not sure I think about it enough.
LENI: I've heard you're too inflexible.
JOSEF K: Who said that?
LENI: Don't be so inflexible. There's no way you can defend
     yourself against this court, you have to admit your guilt,
     that's all. Make a full confession as soon as you can. That's

the only way you can escape from them. And I'm going to
help you. But you have to say my name first.
JOSEF K: Leni.

K pulls her on to his lap.
LENI: Ooh that's nice.

She clasps her arms around his neck.
JOSEF K: And if I don't confess my guilt, then you won't be able
to help me?
LENI: No, then I won't be able to help you. But you don't want
my help at all, do you? You're obstinate and you won't listen
to reason. Aren't you? You're obstinate, aren't you?

She touches his face.
Look. I've got a physical defect.

She spreads two fingers.
Feel it.

He touches a web of skin between her fingers.
JOSEF K: Extraordinary.

He pulls the fingers apart and together a number of times.
What a pretty little paw.

He kisses her fingers.
LENI: You've kissed me!

*She kisses his neck, slips from his lap, he tries to catch her, falls
with her to the floor.*
Now you belong to me!

EXT. HULD'S HOUSE. NIGHT
A stationary cab. Rain.
The house door opens. LENI *and* K.
LENI: Come whenever you want.

She blows a kiss and closes the door.

UNCLE *jumps out of the cab, rushes at* K, *shoves him against the
wall.*
K'S UNCLE: How could you do it? Do you realize the damage
you've done to your case? You sneak off with that dirty little
whore, who is obviously his mistress, you stay away for
hours, and we're all left sitting there – your uncle, your
lawyer and the Clerk of the Court – a man who has complete
authority over your case as it stands at present. They're
polite, they're diplomatic, they don't mention it, they spare

my feelings, but finally they fall silent and we all sit there
looking at each other. Finally the Clerk of the Court gets up,
he says good night and he goes. My friend is dumbstruck, he
can't say a word, you've probably helped give him a
complete breakdown and hastened the death of the man on
whom you are totally dependent. And as for me – I'm soaked
right through, soaked, wet through, soaked to my skin. How
could you do it?
K *is silent.*

INT. BANK: K'S OFFICE. MORNING
K *swivelling slowly in his chair.*
He slowly moves objects from one place to another on his desk.
His arm stretches out on the desk.
He sits quite still, head down.

INT. HULD'S STUDY. DUSK
K *sitting. Huld seated at a very large desk.*
HULD: The proceedings are not public, you see. You must
    remember that. As a result of this, the Court records, above
    all the record of the charge, are not accessible to the accused

or his defence. The consequent problem is that one does not know, or knows very imprecisely, what it is the initial plea has to contest. This does place the defence at a disadvantage, I freely admit. But it is quite deliberate. Defence counsels are not provided for under the law, they profess only on sufferance. The law intends, as far as is possible, to eliminate defence counsel altogether, so that the whole onus is placed on the accused man himself. But it would be quite wrong to infer from this that the defendant does not need a lawyer before this court. On the contrary, in no other court is a lawyer so necessary. And may I say in all humility that you are fortunate in your choice of lawyer. I have excellent contacts and I have already had a number of discussions – with – I must concede – limited success. Some officials have expressed favourable opinions, others much less favourable. The Chief Clerk of the Court, of course, to whom you behaved so unwisely in this very room, refuses, for the time being, to be at all moved by your plight. But on the whole I would say the outlook is moderately cheering. Nothing is totally lost. And if we can win over the Clerk of the Court to our side we can await subsequent developments without any qualms.

JOSEF K: I propose that I write a short account of my life – a survey of my life from every conceivable angle, recalling the minutest actions and events. An onerous task, I agree, but I believe it should be done and that the advantages of such a defence are indisputable. I intend to hand this defence in to the Court myself.

HULD: What you say is madness.

LENI comes into the room with tea for DR HULD. *She gives it to him. She stands behind* K's *chair.* HULD *drinks the tea.* LENI *strokes* K's *hair. They watch* HULD *drink.*

Absolute madness.

INT. HULD'S: THE DARK HALL. DUSK

LENI *and* K *embracing.* LENI *whispers.*

LENI: There's a painter called Titorelli. He paints for the Court. He paints the judges. Go to see him.

She gives him a piece of paper.

INT. BANK: K'S OFFICE. MORNING
K *swivelling slowly in his chair.*
He slowly moves objects from one place to another on his desk.
His arm stretches out on the desk.
He sits quite still, head down.
A knock at the door. The ASSISTANT *enters.* K *stares at him.*
K'S ASSISTANT: I'm sorry Herr K, I know you were not to be
    disturbed but the three gentlemen are still waiting to see
    you. I have told them that you are engaged on especially
    important work, but it is now two hours and they are quite
    distressed –
JOSEF K: I'm going out. My overcoat please.
    He goes to the door.

INT. BANK: ANTE-ROOM AND K'S OFFICE. DAY
The three BUSINESSMEN. *They stand as* K *comes out. The*
ASSISTANT *brings his overcoat.*
FIRST BUSINESSMAN: Herr K, we are really very anxious to
    speak to you –
JOSEF K: You must excuse me, gentlemen, I'm afraid that after
    all I have no time to see you today. I have urgent business
    to attend to. I really must leave at once. Could you possibly
    come back tomorrow? Or perhaps we could talk on the
    telephone.
    The DEPUTY MANAGER *comes into the room.*
DEPUTY MANAGER: So you're going out now, Herr K?
JOSEF K: Yes. I have business. Urgent business.
DEPUTY MANAGER: But these gentlemen have been waiting to
    see you for some considerable time.
JOSEF K: It's all agreed.
SECOND BUSINESSMAN: But I really must protest –
THIRD BUSINESSMAN: We wouldn't have waited all this time
    if –
DEPUTY MANAGER: Gentlemen, there's one very simple
    solution. If you're prepared to make do with me, I should
    be very glad to take over the negotiations in place of the
    Senior Clerk. Of course your business must be discussed
    straight away. Please come into my office.
    The men go out with the DEPUTY MANAGER.

K *leaves the room, stands still for a moment in the corridor, turns,
goes back into his office.*
The DEPUTY MANAGER *is bending over* K's *filing cabinet. He
looks up.*
So you haven't gone yet? I'm looking for the Donner
agreement. Do you know where it is?
K *moves forward.*
It's all right, I've got it.
The DEPUTY MANAGER *goes back to his own office.*

EXT. SLUM DISTRICT. DAY
K *walks down a street.*

EXT. SLUM DISTRICT: TITORELLI'S HOUSE. DAY
K *stands outside a house, checking the address. There is a hole in the
brickwork. A yellow steaming fluid is pouring out of this. Rats by a
drain. At the bottom of the steps a small child lies howling.
On the other side of the front door a tinsmith's workshop. Three
assistants hitting an object with their hammers. A big sheet of tin plate
hanging on a wall reflecting light.*
K *goes into the house.*

INT. TITORELLI'S STAIRWAY. DAY
*Young girls come running out of a flat, laughing, rushing up the stairs.
K follows them. One* GIRL, *slightly hunchbacked, about thirteen years
old, slips on the stairs and then looks up at* K *as he approaches. She
wears a very short skirt.*
JOSEF K: Is there a painter called Titorelli living here?
    *She stands, slides up to him, pokes him in the stomach with her
    elbow.*
    Do you know the painter Titorelli?
    The GIRL *stands even closer to him.*
GIRL: What do you want him for?
JOSEF K: I want him to paint my portrait.
    The GIRL *giggles.*
GIRL: Paint your portrait?
    *She hits him gently, runs up the stairs. He follows.
    She disappears round the next bend in the stairs.* K *turns the
    bend. All the girls are waiting for him, standing on either side of*

the stairs, smoothing their skirts. He passes between them.
They close in behind him. The HUNCHBACK *points him to a very*
narrow wooden staircase. At the top of it is a door made of
boards. The name TITORELLI *is painted on it in red.*
The door is flung open. A man in a nightshirt stands at it.
TITORELLI: (*To* K) Come in, come in.
The girls rush up the stairs and try to push their way in.
TITORELLI *throws them out. The* HUNCHBACK *slips into his*
room.

INT. TITORELLI'S ROOM. DAY
K *goes in.* TITORELLI *whirls the* HUNCHBACK *around and dumps her*
outside the door. He shuts the door.
TITORELLI: I am the painter Titorelli.
JOSEF K: You seem to be very popular.
TITORELLI: Oh, those girls! They're a damn nuisance. They get
everywhere. Last night I found one of them under my bed.
The girls start to scratch on the walls. They can be glimpsed
through the cracks in the wood.
VOICE: Titorelli, can we come in now?
TITORELLI: No!
VOICE: What about me? Just me?
TITORELLI: I said no!
K *looks at an easel covered by a shirt, sleeves dangling.*
JOSEF K: A girl called Leni gave me your name.
TITORELLI: I know Leni.
JOSEF K: She says you are trusted by the Court.
TITORELLI: I am certainly trusted by the Court. She's quite
right. I take it you are an accused man?
JOSEF K: Yes. I am.
TITORELLI: And you would like some help from me?
JOSEF K: If that's possible.
TITORELLI: Let me ask you one question. Are you innocent?
JOSEF K: Yes. I am completely innocent.
TITORELLI: I see. Well, if you're innocent, the whole thing is
very simple.
JOSEF K: Is it?
TITORELLI: Yes, yes of course. But you are definitely innocent?
JOSEF K: Definitely.

TITORELLI: Well, that's the main thing.
Girls scratching on the wall.
JOSEF K: But I understand that once the Court has made an indictment, it is firmly convinced that the accused is guilty and it can be budged from that conviction only with great difficulty.
TITORELLI: With great difficulty? It can't be budged at all. The Court can never be budged.
VOICE: Titorelli, is he going to go soon?
TITORELLI: Shut up!
VOICE: Are you going to paint him? Don't paint him! He's so ugly.
TITORELLI: If you don't keep quiet, I'll throw you all down the stairs.
He whispers in K's ear.
Those girls belong to the Court too.
JOSEF K: Oh, do they?
TITORELLI: You don't seem to know much about the Court, do you? But since you're innocent, you won't need to. I can get you off by myself.
JOSEF K: How? You said yourself the Court can never be budged.
TITORELLI: Not head on, no. But it's different behind the scenes, in the corridors, in this room, for example. You see, I know them all, well, not all, but quite a few. I inherited this post. My father was the Court painter before me. It's a position handed on from father to son, you see. And every judge wants to be painted just as the grand old judges were in the old days, and there's no one else who can do that except me. Do you understand?
JOSEF K: So your position is unassailable?
TITORELLI: Unassailable. Now, our aim is to get you acquitted, right? So I have to ask you first what kind of acquittal you want. There are three possibilities. Actual acquittal, ostensible acquittal and indefinite postponement.
Actual acquittal is, naturally, the best, but I haven't the slightest influence on that kind of verdict. Nobody has. And to be quite frank, I have to tell you I've never come across a single case of actual acquittal in my whole life.
JOSEF K: What about in years gone by?

TITORELLI: Oh, there are stories of such acquittals – but they're very hard to prove. The Court's final verdicts are never published, you see, they're not even available to the judges, so only legends about old legal cases have come down to us. The majority of these legends are in fact describing cases of actual acquittal – you can believe them if you like, but you can't prove them. Some of them are in fact very beautiful, very tender, inspiring.

JOSEF K: But you can't cite these legends as evidence before the Court, I take it?

TITORELLI *laughs*.

TITORELLI: No. You can't.

JOSEF K: Then let's stop talking about 'actual acquittal'. Tell me about the two other courses.

TITORELLI: Ostensible acquittal and indefinite postponement. Why don't you take your jacket off? You look hot.

JOSEF K: Yes, it's unbearable. Can't you open a window?

TITORELLI: It won't open. But lots of air comes through the cracks.

JOSEF K: I'll take off my jacket.

Girls' voices.

GIRLS: He's taken off his jacket!

TITORELLI: Shut up! Right, let's take ostensible acquittal first. What happens is this – I write out a statement of your innocence. The text for this has been handed down by my father, by the way, and is unimpeachable. With this statement I go the rounds of the judges. I might begin with the judge I'm painting at the moment, for example. I explain that you're innocent and I offer to guarantee your innocence myself.

JOSEF K: And will he believe you?

TITORELLI: Not every judge will believe me, but once I get a sufficient number of judges to countersign the statement, I take it to the judge who is actually conducting your trial. This judge has the guarantee of a number of his colleagues, so he can order the acquittal with an easy mind and you walk out of the court a free man.

JOSEF K: A free man.

TITORELLI: Yes. But only ostensibly free. You see, my judges are

the lowest grade of judges, they don't have the right to give a
final, an actual acquittal. Only the very highest court, which
is absolutely inaccessible to you, to me, and to all of us, can
do that. You see, the difference between actual and
ostensible acquittal can be demonstrated in a purely external
way.
With actual acquittal all the documents are set aside. They
vanish. The trial is deleted, as it were. With ostensible
acquittal, the case records remain in circulation and one day
some judge or other comes across them, looks through them,
realizes the charge is still valid and orders an immediate
arrest.

JOSEF K: And the trial begins again.

TITORELLI: The trial begins again. But of course there's always
the chance of obtaining another ostensible acquittal.

JOSEF K: But that second acquittal isn't final?

TITORELLI: No, no. It's ostensible. It can be followed by a third
arrest, a third acquittal, a fourth arrest, a fourth acquittal
and so on, *ad infinitum.*
He studies K.
So how do you like the sound of ostensible acquittal?

JOSEF K: Tell me about the other one.

TITORELLI: Indefinite postponement. (*He thinks.*) That consists
in preventing the trial from advancing beyond its earliest
stages. To achieve this, the defendant and his helper must
keep in constant contact with the Court. You mustn't lose
sight of your case for a moment, you have to keep the case
revolving in the same small circle, you must submit yourself
for regular interrogation, visit all the judges who can
influence your own, keep the case from progressing, you see,
by acting with unswerving persistence and vigilance – but of
course there's no rest, there's no sleep, it can go on for ever,
you can never, as they say, drop your guard –
K *stands.*

GIRLS: He's up!

TITORELLI: Are you going? Is it the air? I'm so sorry. There's lots
more I wanted to say to you. I had to be quite brief. But I
hope I've made myself understood?

JOSEF K: Oh yes.

TITORELLI: Both methods have this in common – they prevent
      the accused man from being sentenced.
JOSEF K: But they don't ensure any real acquittal.
TITORELLI: You've grasped the crux of the matter.
JOSEF K: You've been kind.
      He goes towards the door.
TITORELLI: You don't want to be pestered by those girls, do you?
      Use this door.
      He climbs over the bed and unlocks another door.
      Don't be afraid to climb over the bed, everybody does it.
      K climbs on to the bed and suddenly sees through the open door.
      He stares.
JOSEF K: What's this?
TITORELLI: This? It's the Court offices. Why are you so
      surprised?

INT. COURT OFFICES. DAY
K's point of view.
Benches in the Court offices corridor. A man sitting, his head in his
hands. Another man standing in the half darkness.

INT. TITORELLI'S ROOM. DAY
K climbs across the bed.

INT. COURT OFFICES. DAY
K staggering, a handkerchief pressed to his mouth.
The girls rush to meet TITORELLI. *They seize his hands, hold on to*
him. TITORELLI *laughs.*
TITORELLI: Can't come any further, I'm afraid! Cheerio! And
      don't be too long thinking it over.
      K staggers down the corridor.

EXT. STREET NEAR HULD'S HOUSE. NIGHT
K walking purposefully towards Dr Huld's house.

EXT. DR HULD'S FRONT DOOR. NIGHT
K rings the bell. Silence. He rings it again. Two eyes at the peephole.
The eyes withdraw. K bangs on the door. Silence.

The door suddenly opens. K *falls in. He glimpses* LENI *in a chemise running down the passage. By the wall stands a skinny little man in shirt sleeves.*
JOSEF K: Do you work here?
BLOCK: I'm a client. I'm here on legal business.

INT. HULD'S: CORRIDOR. NIGHT
K *passes* BLOCK *and turns to study him.*
JOSEF K: Oh yes? She's your mistress, isn't she?
BLOCK: Good God no!
JOSEF K: What's your name?
BLOCK: Block. I'm a businessman.
JOSEF K: Where's Leni? Where's she hiding?
BLOCK: She's probably gone to the kitchen to make soup for the
    lawyer.
JOSEF K: Where's the kitchen? Take me there.

INT. HULD'S: THE KITCHEN. NIGHT
LENI *making soup. She wears an apron.* K *and* BLOCK *come in.*
LENI: Good evening, Josef.
JOSEF K: Good evening.
    He goes to her.
    Who is this man?
LENI: Oh, he's just Block.
JOSEF K: You were in your chemise. Is he your lover? Answer
    me.
LENI: Come into the other room and I'll explain everything.
JOSEF K: No. Explain here.
    She tries to kiss him. He stops her.
    Is he your lover?
LENI: Josef, you're not going to be jealous of Block? (*To* BLOCK)
    Rudi, I'm under suspicion. Say something.
BLOCK: (*To* JOSEF K) It beats me how you can be jealous of me.
JOSEF K: Yes, it beats me too.
    LENI *laughs.*
LENI: Do you want to see the lawyer? Shall I announce you first
    or take him his soup first?
JOSEF K: Announce me first.
    LENI *goes out. He calls her back.*

Take him his soup first.

LENI *goes to the stove.*

LENI: Then I'll take him his soup. The only trouble is, he may fall asleep. He never takes long to fall asleep after his soup.

JOSEF K: What I have to say to him will keep him awake.

LENI: The minute he's had his soup I'll tell him you're here, so I can have you back with me as soon as possible.

JOSEF K: Oh, go and give him his soup. Get on with it.

LENI: Do be nicer. Please.

She goes out with the soup. K *and* BLOCK *are silent.* K *walks up and down the kitchen.* BLOCK *watches him.*

BLOCK: I've seen you before. I saw you in the Court offices some time ago.

JOSEF K: Oh. Did you?

BLOCK: I was sitting in the passage when you went through.

JOSEF K: Yes. I was there – some time ago.

BLOCK: I'm there practically every day.

JOSEF K: Tell me. Do you remember that everyone stood up when I came in? Why did they do that? Did they think I was a judge?

BLOCK: No no, not at all, We were standing up for the usher. We knew you were an accused man.

JOSEF K: Oh. But then, perhaps my behaviour struck you as arrogant?

BLOCK: On the contrary.

JOSEF K: What do you mean?

BLOCK: The Court is full of superstitions. One of these superstitions going the rounds is that you can tell from the defendant's face – particularly from the outline of his lips – what the outcome of his case is going to be. Well, those people there on that day maintained that – judging by your lips – you were certain to be convicted, and pretty soon at that. So we didn't think you were arrogant, we thought you were deluded. And so we felt pity for you.

JOSEF K: My lips! I can't see anything special about my lips. Can you?

BLOCK: Absolutely nothing at all.

JOSEF K: Superstitious rubbish.

LENI *comes back into the kitchen. She looks at them and laughs.*

LENI: Aren't you sitting close together, you two? Like old pals.
She takes the candle from BLOCK, *wipes his hand with her apron
and kneels down to scrape grease off his trousers.*
JOSEF K: What are you doing?
LENI: Cleaning him up. The lawyer is waiting for you. Why don't
you go in? We've got to clean Block up for his bedtime.
JOSEF K: Bedtime? What bedtime?
LENI: Block's bedtime. He often sleeps here, don't you?
JOSEF K: He *sleeps* here?
LENI: Not everyone's like you, Josef, allowed in to see the lawyer
any time they like. Look! It's eleven o'clock and the lawyer is
happy to see you. Block's not so lucky. Are you? You know,
sometimes I announce him and he doesn't get in to see the
lawyer until three days later. And if he isn't on the spot when
he's called for he has to be announced all over again.
That's why I've let him sleep here, because it's even happened
that the lawyer has rung for him in the middle of the night.
K *looks at* BLOCK.
BLOCK: As time goes by, one becomes very dependent on one's
lawyer.
JOSEF K: How much time has gone by, in your case?
BLOCK: Five years. It's been going on for over five years.
LENI: He loves sleeping here. Don't you? Would you like to see his
bedroom?
She opens a door off the kitchen. K *looks in. The room is
windowless, tiny, filled by a narrow bed. A niche in the wall holds
a candle, an inkwell and a pen. Piles of papers sit on the bed.*
JOSEF K: (*To* BLOCK) So you sleep in the maid's room?
BLOCK: That's right.
JOSEF K: (*To* LENI) Oh, get him to bed!
LENI: I hope you're not going to be in such a bad temper with the
lawyer.
JOSEF K: Bad temper? Not at all. I'm simply going to tell him that
I'm dismissing him.
BLOCK: He's dismissing him!
BLOCK *rushes round and round the kitchen.*
He's dismissing the lawyer! Oh my God! He's dismissing the
lawyer!
LENI *runs at* K. BLOCK *and* LENI *collide. She strikes him.*

INT. HULD'S: THE CORRIDOR. NIGHT
K *runs up the corridor towards the bedroom.* LENI *chases him.*
K *opens the bedroom door.* LENI *puts her foot in the door, tries to pull
him back.* K *twists her wrist violently. She cries out. He pushes her
away, goes into the bedroom, shuts and locks the door.*

INT. HULD'S BEDROOM. NIGHT
DR HULD *is sitting up in bed.*
HULD: I've been waiting for you.
JOSEF K: I'm going in a moment.
HULD: I shan't let you in another time as late as this.
JOSEF K: That suits me.
    Pause.
HULD: Sit down.
JOSEF K: If you wish me to.
    He sits.
HULD: Did I see you lock the door?
JOSEF K: Yes. That was because of Leni.
HULD: Is she pestering you? (*He laughs.*) It's such a strange quirk
    she has. She just finds accused men wildly attractive. She
    can't help running after them. She falls in love with them all
    and indeed they all seem to fall in love with her. Even that
    miserable worm Block she finds attractive – just because he's
    an accused man.
    Pause.
    What do you think about that?
JOSEF K: Nothing.
    Pause.
HULD: Did you come here tonight to see me for any particular
    reason?
JOSEF K: Yes. I came to tell you that I'm taking my defence out of
    your hands, as from today.
    HULD *stares at him.*
HULD: Do I understand you correctly?
JOSEF K: I trust you do. I've been thinking about this for a long
    time. My decision is final.
    HULD *pushes the quilt back and sits on the edge of the bed.*
    You'll get a chill.
    HULD *wraps the quilt around him.*

HULD: Your uncle is a friend of mine and I've also become fond of
    you in the course of time. I admit it quite openly. I don't
    need to be ashamed of it.
JOSEF K: Let me make myself clear. I believe it is necessary to
    take much more drastic measures in this case than have been
    taken up to now.
HULD: You are impatient.
JOSEF K: No, it's not a matter of impatience. The case is closing
    in on me more and more. I am being slowly poisoned.
HULD: You know, I once saw beautifully expressed in a book the
    difference which obtains between legal representation in
    ordinary actions and legal representation in cases like this.
    This is what it said: in the first, the lawyer leads his client by
    a thread until the verdict is reached; in the second, he
    straightaway lifts his client on to his shoulder and carries
    him, without putting him down, as far as the verdict and
    beyond. And that is the truth. To be defence counsel in a
    case of this nature is a great and noble task, a task which I
    have never for a moment regretted, except perhaps now,
    when I find my work so completely misunderstood.
    Silence.
    Let me say this. I get the impression that what has misled
    you into misjudging my legal assistance is that you have been
    treated too well. I'd like to show you how other accused men
    are treated – perhaps you'll manage to learn something from
    it. I'm going to send for Block now, so kindly unlock the
    door.
    *K remains still for a moment. He then goes to the door, unlocks it
    and sits again.*
    HULD rings a bell. LENI comes in immediately.
    Bring Block here.
    LENI calls down the corridor.
LENI: Block! The lawyer wants you!
    HULD gets back on to the bed and turns to the wall.
    LENI slides behind K's chair and caresses him.
    BLOCK appears in the doorway. He enters cautiously.
    HULD speaks from beneath the quilt.
HULD: Is Block there?
BLOCK: At your service.

HULD: What do you want? You've come at an inopportune
    moment.
BLOCK: Wasn't I called for?
HULD: Yes, you were called for. But you've come at an
    inopportune moment.
    Pause.
    You always do.
BLOCK: Do you want me to go away?
HULD: You may stay, as you're here.
    Pause.
    Yesterday I was with the Third Judge. He's a friend of mine.
    I gradually got the conversation on to you. Do you want to
    know what he said?
BLOCK: Oh, please.
    BLOCK *bows as if about to go down on his knees.*
    Oh, please.
JOSEF K: (*To* BLOCK) What in God's name are you doing?
    LENI *puts her hand over* K's *mouth. He seizes both her hands and
    holds them tight.*
    BLOCK *kneels by the bed.*
BLOCK: I'm kneeling, Dr Huld.
    He strokes the quilt. LENI *frees herself from* K. *She sits on the
    edge of the bed and looks down at* BLOCK. *He looks up at her
    imploringly, glancing at* DR HULD. *She mimes kissing* DR
    HULD's *hand.*
    BLOCK *takes* DR HULD's *hand and kisses it, twice.* HULD *does
    not move.*
    LENI *bends over* HULD *and strokes his hair.*
HULD: How has he been behaving himself today?
LENI: He's been quiet and industrious.
HULD: What's he been doing?
LENI: Well, so that he wouldn't disturb my work, I locked him in
    his room. I peeped through the gap in the door every so
    often. He was always kneeling on the bed reading the papers
    you gave him. He was reading all day. He was doing his best.
    I know he was. It wasn't until eight o'clock that I let him out
    and gave him something to eat.
HULD: You're praising him – which makes it even more difficult
    for me to say what I have to say.

What the Judge said was not favourable.

LENI: Not favourable?

HULD: Not favourable.

LENI: But how can that be?

HULD: He didn't even like it when I started to talk about Block.
'Don't talk to me about Block,' he said. 'But he's my client,'
I said. 'You're wasting your time,' the Judge said. I said, 'Of
course personally he's quite awful, his manners are horrible
and he's dirty, but as far as organizing a legal case is
concerned, he's irreproachable.' I was exaggerating on
purpose. But to no avail. I am now forced to repeat what the
Judge then said.

HULD *looks at* BLOCK *for the first time.*

'Block is cunning,' he said. 'He knows how to drag his case
out. But his ignorance is much greater than his cunning.
What would he say, do you think, if he found out that his
trial has not even begun yet, that the signal to begin it has not
even been given?'

BLOCK's *face aghast.*

K *looks on, impassive.*

INT. K'S SITTING ROOM. NIGHT
K *sitting still. A knock on the door.*
FRAU GRUBACH: (*Out of shot*) Herr K, there is a telephone call for
    you.
    K *slowly looks up. He stands and goes to the door.*

INT. GRUBACH'S HALL. NIGHT
K *goes to the telephone.*
JOSEF K: Josef K.
MANAGER'S VOICE: Herr K. This is Herr Deimen. (*Pause.*)
    From the bank.
JOSEF K: Oh, good evening, Herr Deimen.
MANAGER: You know of course the Italian firm Sitari?
JOSEF K: I do, yes.
MANAGER: Their chairman is arriving here tonight on business.
    But he's very eager to see some of our art museums and
    monuments – that sort of thing – in the morning. I'd be so
    grateful to you if you would act as his guide. I mean, you
    know about art and you speak Italian. Could you possibly
    spare a couple of hours?
JOSEF K: Of course, Herr Diemen.
MANAGER: Wonderful. He wants an early start. Eight o'clock suit
    you?
JOSEF K: Certainly.
MANAGER: Thank you so much. I'll see you in the reception
    room.
    K *replaces the receiver and stands.*
    FRAU GRUBACH *is looking at him through a chink in the kitchen
    door.*

INT. K'S BEDROOM. NIGHT
K *lying in his bed in moonlight. His eyes are wide open.*

INT. BANK: RECEPTION ROOM. MORNING
K *enters the room. The* MANAGER *and the* ITALIAN *are sitting in
armchairs. They stand. The* MANAGER *introduces* K *to the* ITALIAN.
MANAGER: Signor Rossi has just been telling me that he doesn't
    actually have as much time as he'd hoped. He'll have to
    restrict his sightseeing. I've suggested you simply show him

round the Cathedral. Do you think that's a good idea?

JOSEF K: Yes indeed.

The MANAGER *looks at his watch.*

MANAGER: He has an appointment now – so he would like to meet you at the Cathedral at ten o'clock. Is that convenient?

JOSEF K: Of course.

ROSSI: (*To* JOSEF K) I am very grateful to you. I look forward immensely to seeing you at the Cathedral at ten o'clock.
They all shake hands. ROSSI *goes.*

MANAGER: I'm also very grateful to you. But simply confining things to the Cathedral won't be so demanding, will it? He's a very important client, as you know.

INT. BANK: ANTE-ROOM. DAY

K *walking through the room. The telephone rings. He picks it up.*

JOSEF K: Josef K.

LENI'S VOICE: It's Leni. How are you?

JOSEF K: Oh . . . I have to meet an Italian at the Cathedral . . . later this morning.

LENI: The Cathedral?

JOSEF K: Yes, the Cathedral.

LENI: But why the Cathedral?
Silence.
They're hounding you.
K *puts the phone down. He stands still. He murmurs.*

JOSEF K: Yes, they're hounding me.

EXT. CATHEDRAL. DAY

It is raining. The clock is striking ten.

K *walking across the square towards the main entrance.*

He looks about him. ROSSI *nowhere to be seen.*

K *walks to a side entrance. No sign of* ROSSI.

K *walking round the Cathedral. Various doors are closed.*

K *walks back to the main entrance. The clock says ten-twenty.* K *looks about. There is no sign of* ROSSI. K *enters the Cathedral.*

INT. CATHEDRAL. DAY

K *goes to the bookstall. He looks through various guidebooks. An* ATTENDANT *is counting change.*

JOSEF K: Which would you say is the most reliable guide to the
  Cathedral?
ATTENDANT: This one.
JOSEF K: Thank you. How much is this?
ATTENDANT: One krone.

K gives her a note.

JOSEF K: Thank you.

He walks into the Cathedral and sits down in a pew.
*He opens the guidebook and glances through it. He blinks, looks
up.*
*In the distance, on the high altar, a great triangle of candle flames
is sparkling. K puts the book down and stands up.*
*He walks towards the pulpit. A fat candle is burning on a pillar.
Suddenly he turns. A man is watching him in the distance. He
appears to be a VERGER. He points vaguely to something behind
K , nodding his head.*

What do you want?

*He moves towards the VERGER. The VERGER waves him away
and limps off.*
*K follows the VERGER and then stops. When K stops, the
VERGER stops. The VERGER turns and points, as before.*
K shrugs and walks back towards his pew.
*He is suddenly aware of a small side pulpit, with a lamp on. A
PRIEST is standing at the foot of it. His hand is on the rail. He is
staring at K. He nods at him. K crosses himself and bows. The
PRIEST climbs up to the pulpit.*
*K looks at his watch in the dim light. Eleven a.m. The PRIEST
tests the lamp on the pulpit. He screws it tighter.*
*K starts to walk back towards the entrance. He passes empty
pews. There is no one at all in the Cathedral. He finds his pew.
He picks up the guidebook and moves to the door.*

PRIEST'S VOICE: Josef K!

K stops. He stares at the ground.
He looks up at the door in front of him.
Silence.
*He turns his head slightly and looks back at the PRIEST. The
PRIEST is standing quite calmly, in the pulpit.*
K turns round. The PRIEST beckons to him.
K suddenly runs towards the pulpit. He stops before he reaches it.

The PRIEST *points to a spot just below the pulpit.* K *walks to it.*
PRIEST: You are Josef K?
JOSEF K: Yes.
PRIEST: You are an accused man.
JOSEF K: Yes. So I've been informed.
PRIEST: Then you're the man I'm looking for. I am the Prison
    Chaplain.
JOSEF K: Oh, are you?
PRIEST: I had you summoned here – to have a talk with you.
JOSEF K: No, no. That's not accurate. I came here to show an
    Italian round the Cathedral.
PRIEST: Keep to the point. What's that you have in your hand? Is
    it a prayer book?
JOSEF K: No. It's a guidebook to this Cathedral.
PRIEST: Put it down.
    K *throws it away violently. It skids, twists, and comes apart on
    the Cathedral floor.*
    Do you know that your case is going badly?
JOSEF K: I have that impression.
PRIEST: How do you think it will end?
JOSEF K: I don't know. Do you?
PRIEST: No, but I fear it will end badly. Your case may not get
    beyond a lower court. You are considered to be guilty.
JOSEF K: But I am not. And anyway, how can any man be called
    guilty? We're all human beings, aren't we? One human being
    is just like another.
PRIEST: That's true, but that's how all guilty men speak.
JOSEF K: So you're prejudiced against me too?
PRIEST: No, I'm not prejudiced against you.
JOSEF K: Thank you. But people are prejudiced against me. My
    position is becoming more and more difficult.
PRIEST: You don't seem to understand the essential facts. The
    verdict does not come all at once. The proceedings gradually
    merge into the verdict.
    Pause.
JOSEF K: So that's how it is.
    Pause.
PRIEST: What do you plan to do next?
JOSEF K: Get more help.

PRIEST: You ask for too much help from other people. Especially
     women. Don't you see that's not the kind of help you need?
JOSEF K: Oh, I don't know. Women have great power. And this
     court is obsessed by women. Show an examining magistrate
     an attractive woman in the distance and he'll knock over his
     table and the defendant in order to get his hands on her.
     The PRIEST *leans over the balustrade and stares down at him.*
     In background the VERGER *is putting out candles.*
     Are you angry with me? Perhaps you don't realize the kind of
     court you're serving?
     Pause.
     I'm only telling you what I've observed.
     Pause.
     I didn't mean to offend you.
     The PRIEST *raises his voice.*
PRIEST: Can't you see what is going to happen to you? Can't you
     see what is staring you in the face?
     Silence.
JOSEF K: Won't you come down here? You haven't got to preach
     a sermon. Can you come down?
PRIEST: Yes, I can come down now. I had to speak to you first
     from a distance – because – you see – I am quite easily
     influenced and tend to forget my duty.
     He detaches the lamp from the hook on the pulpit, climbs down,
     and gives the lamp to K.
JOSEF K: Can you spare me a little more time?
PRIEST: As much as you need.
JOSEF K: You're being very kind to me. I appreciate it. You're an
     exception among those who belong to the Court. I trust you
     more than any of them. I feel I can speak freely to you.

INT. CATHEDRAL: DARK AISLE. NIGHT
They walk up and down the dark aisle, side by side.
PRIEST: Don't delude yourself.
JOSEF K: How am I deluding myself?
PRIEST: You're deluding yourself about the Court. In the
     writings which preface the Law it says about this delusion:
     Before the Law stands a door-keeper. A man from the
     country comes up to this door-keeper and begs for admission

to the Law. But the door-keeper tells him that he cannot
grant him admission now. The man ponders this and then
asks if he will be allowed to enter later. 'Possibly,' the
door-keeper says, 'but not now.' Since the door leading to
the Law is standing open as always and the door-keeper steps
aside, the man looks through the door. Seeing this, the
door-keeper laughs and says: 'If it attracts you so much, go
on and try to get in without my permission. But you must
realize that I am powerful. And I'm only the lowest door-
keeper. At every hall there is another door-keeper, each one
more powerful than the last. Even I cannot bear to look at
the third one.'
The man from the country had not expected difficulties like
this, for, he thinks, the Law is surely supposed to be
accessible to everyone always, but when he looks more
closely at the door-keeper in his fur coat, with his great sharp
nose and his long, thin black Tartar beard, he decides it is
better to wait until he receives permission to enter. The
door-keeper gives him a stool and allows him to sit down to
one side of the door. There he sits, day after day, and year
after year.

During all these long years, the man watches the door-keeper
almost continuously. He forgets the other door-keepers, this
first one seems to be the only obstacle between him and
admission to the Law. In the first years he curses his ill-luck
aloud, but later when he gets old, he only grumbles to
himself. He becomes childish and, since he has been
scrutinizing the door-keeper so closely for years that he can
identify even the fleas in the door-keeper's fur collar, he begs
these fleas to help him to change the door-keeper's mind.
In the end his eyes grow dim and he cannot tell whether it is
really getting darker around him or whether it is just his eyes
deceiving him.
But now he glimpses in the darkness a radiance glowing
inextinguishably from the door of the Law. He is not going
to live much longer now. Before he dies all his experiences
during the whole period of waiting merge in his head into
one single question, which he has not yet asked the door-
keeper. As he can no longer raise his stiffening body, he
beckons the man over. The door-keeper has to bend down
low to him, for the difference in size between them has
changed very much to the man's disadvantage.
'What is it you want to know now then?' asks the door-
keeper. 'You're insatiable.' 'All men are intent on the Law,'
says the man, 'but why is it that in all these many years no
one other than myself has asked to enter through this door?'
The door-keeper realizes that the man is nearing his end and
that his hearing is fading, and in order to make himself heard
he bellows at him: 'No one else could gain admission through
this door, because this door was intended only for you. I
shall now go and shut it.'
They walk on.
JOSEF K: The door-keeper deceived the man.
PRIEST: Don't be too hasty.
JOSEF K: It's obvious. The door-keeper didn't tell the man the
    truth until it was too late.
PRIEST: He wasn't asked the question until then. And remember
    he was only a door-keeper.
JOSEF K: But he had power! And he used it to destroy the man.
    He's a criminal. He should have been dismissed.

PRIEST: But you've missed the point. The scripture is
    unalterable.
    K *stops and stares at him.*
    The PRIEST *walks on.* K *follows.*
    They walk on in silence.
JOSEF K: Aren't we near the main entrance?
PRIEST: No. We're a long way away. Why? Do you want to go
    now?
JOSEF K: Yes of course I want to go. I have to go. I'm a senior
    clerk at a bank. They're expecting me. I only came here to
    show a business associate from abroad around the
    Cathedral.
    The PRIEST *holds out his hand.*
PRIEST: Well then, go.
JOSEF K: I don't think I can find my way alone in the dark.
PRIEST: Just keep to the wall on your left, keep right along that
    wall and you'll find a door.
    The PRIEST *withdraws.*
JOSEF K: Wait! Please! Wait!
    The PRIEST *turns.*
PRIEST: I'm waiting.
    Pause.
JOSEF K: Don't you want to hear anything more from me?
PRIEST: No.
JOSEF K: But you were being so kind to me, explaining things to
    me, now you're letting me go as if you cared nothing about
    me.
PRIEST: But it was you who said you had to go.
JOSEF K: Yes, you must understand that.
PRIEST: But you must understand what I am also.
JOSEF K: You're the Prison Chaplain.
PRIEST: Precisely. That means I belong to the Court. So why
    should I want anything from you? The Court doesn't want
    anything from you. It receives you when you come and it
    dismisses you when you go.

INT. K'S SITTING ROOM. NINE O'CLOCK. NIGHT
K *sitting still.*
A ring at the front door. The door opens, closes.

Footsteps.
A knock on the door. The door opens. Two MEN *come in. They are*
portly, formally but shabbily dressed.
K *stands up.*
JOSEF K: You've come for me.
> The MEN *nod.*
> K *goes to the window and looks out.*

WINDOW OPPOSITE. K'S POINT OF VIEW. NIGHT
In a lighted window across the street babies are playing in playpens,
stretching their hands out between the bars.

INT. K'S SITTING ROOM AND BEDROOM. NIGHT
K *turns and looks at the two* MEN, *who stand patiently, holding their*
hats.
K *mutters to himself.*
JOSEF K: So they send old ham actors for me. They're trying to
> get rid of me on the cheap. (*To the* MEN) What theatre are
> you playing at?
FIRST MAN: Theatre?
> *They look at each other.*
JOSEF K: Oh well, let's get on with it.

INT. GRUBACH'S HALL. NIGHT
K *goes out of the room. The two* MEN *follow. He gets his hat from the*
hall. They go out.

EXT. GRUBACH'S HOUSE. NIGHT
They come out of the house. The MEN *link arms with* K.
They walk, passing from the light of street lamp into shadow, into light
and into shadow.
K *looks from left to right at their heavy double chins.*

EXT. A DESERTED SQUARE. NIGHT
The square is decorated with flower beds. The three come into the
square. K *suddenly stops.*
JOSEF K: Why the hell did they have to send you, of all people!
> *The* MEN *are passive. They stand holding on to* K.
> Well, that's it. I won't go any further.

They try to hoist K *from the spot. He resists, simply by rooting himself to the ground.*
You're going to have a hard job of it, you know.
Suddenly he sees FRÄULEIN BÜRSTNER *at the corner of the square, climbing up a small flight of steps. She is caught in the moonlight.* K *stops resisting. The* MEN *look at him, relax. He begins to walk in the direction of* FRÄULEIN BÜRSTNER, *the* MEN *with him.*
FRÄULEIN BÜRSTNER *disappears.* K *speaks, half to the* MEN, *half to himself.*

JOSEF K: Yes, all I can do now, you see, yes that's absolutely right, all I can do now is to keep my mind calm and discriminating. I'm not going to leave this life like a raging idiot. Why should I? How can I put it? I don't want people to say of me that at the beginning of my case I wanted it to finish and at the end of it I wanted it to start all over again. Do I? Do you follow? I don't want that to be said. And frankly, I'm very grateful that you two half-dumb imbeciles have been sent to escort me. I'm grateful that it's been left to me to tell myself all that needs to be said.

EXT. BRIDGE. NIGHT
They walk on to a bridge in the moonlight.
A POLICEMAN *appears. He looks at them. The two* MEN *stop. The* POLICEMAN *walks slowly towards them. The policeman is about to speak when* K *abruptly propels them on over the bridge.*
K *looks back. The* POLICEMAN *is looking after them. They turn a corner.*

EXT. DESERTED STREET. NIGHT
K *runs. The* MEN *are forced to run with him.*

EXT. FIELDS AND QUARRY. NIGHT
They walk through fields and arrive at a small quarry. The MEN *stop. They let go of* K.
K *stands still.*
The MEN *wipe their brows.*
Moonlight. The FIRST MAN *goes to* K, *takes off his coat, waistcoat and shirt. He folds the clothes.* K *stands shivering.*

The SECOND MAN *is looking about the quarry. He turns and waves.*
The FIRST MAN *leads* K *to a spot near the wall.*
They lie him down.
They try to fit him comfortably between boulders.
The FIRST MAN *takes out a butcher's knife, holds it, examines the edges.*
The FIRST MAN *hands the knife across* K*'s chest to the* SECOND MAN, *who hands it back.*
K *watches the knife.*
The FIRST MAN *hands the knife across* K*'s chest to the* SECOND MAN, *who hands it back.*
K *looks beyond them to the top storey of a house.*
A window opens. A light flashes on. A figure leans a long way out, stretching out its arms.
K *raises his hands towards the figure, spreading his fingers.*
The FIRST MAN *grasps* K*'s throat. The* SECOND MAN *drives the knife into his heart.*
K *looks up at the dim faces above him, as they look down at him, their cheeks touching.*
JOSEF K: Like a dog!